GW00493093

The Illustrated Guide to

EDIBLE PLANTS

PUBLISHER'S NOTE

This book contains information on a wide range of plants, some of which are, or can be used in the treatment of human disorders. It is primarily intended to be read as a source of interesting information and not as a practical guide to self-medication.

It cannot be over-emphasized that many plants are poisonous, some extremely so, and some which are beneficial in small doses can also be harmful if taken to excess or for long periods. In some cases only part of the plant may be used as a foodstuff. It is for this reason careful reading of the textual information is recommended. Plants which may have unpleasant effects in specific circumstances appear with a warning at the end of the text. It must also be emphasized that under no circumstances should children be involved in the collection or handling of wild plants for the reasons stated. As a general rule, it is recommended that all herbal infusions and decoctions should be freshly prepared and should certainly be used within twelve hours of making up. We should like to stress that the use of any plant or derivative is entirely at the reader's own risk and we hereby disclaim all legal responsibility for any harmful or unwanted effects that might arise from such use.

The Illustrated Guide to
EDIBLE PLANTS

DAGMAR LÁNSKÁ

Illustrations by
PAVEL ŽILÁK

CHANCELLOR PRESS

Translated by Daniela Coxon
Graphic design by Eva Adamcová
Designed and produced by Aventinum for
Chancellor Press
Michelin House, 81 Fulham Road
London SW3 6RB

ISBN 1 85152 117 8
Printed in Czechoslovakia by Svoboda
3/15/30/51-01

CONTENTS

INTRODUCTION

Improved varieties of vegetables and fruit, it may be argued, are more attractive, better tasting and more easily attainable. However, nowadays the number of people interested in food prepared from wild plants is on the increase. In spring, those interested in healthy eating may collect the young vitamin and mineral enriched leaves and shoots of plants as part of a cleansing diet.

In prehistoric times man supplemented his diet of wild animals by collecting leaves, roots, shoots, tubers and fruits. In the beginning he only collected plants, but later in the early neolithic period he began to cultivate and adapt those he most liked and which were apparently of benefit to his health. Plants provide man with basic nutrients, that is proteins, sugars and fats. They are a source of vitamins, minerals, fibre, oils and a number of other protective and medicinal substances. Many wild plants may be used to replace vegetables, others herbs, and whilst not usually very high in calories, they supply us with a number of the substances necessary for healthy living. We also benefit from improved digestion, appetite and metabolism.

Here is a choice of the best known and most appetizing wild plants. In addition to these, many other edible species do exist. Teas, syrups and wines are produced from the flowers of the deadnettle, clover, false locust, meadowsweet, primrose and others. Spring herb soups and salads can be made from the stalks and young leaves of purslane, cress, comfrey, mallow, mint, chicory, deadnettle and silverweed. The boiled roots and tubers of the wild carrot, parsnip, earth-nut pea or lesser celandine can be used as root vegetables. The choice of wild plants is extremely rich and varies according to specific regions. However, this book does not touch upon the so-called 'marginal' foods which are used in times of famine, such as the ground young bark of the birch and oak trees, ground catkins, lichen etc. There are probably many such possibilities which will never be used to the full. It must be emphasized at this point that along with the fact that there are many and varied nourishing and healing plants in the wild, there are also a number of poisonous plants. Never pick or eat a plant about which you are not entirely sure. Some poisonous plants can be mistaken for innocent ones, with most unfortunate effects. It is also probably not a good idea to allow a child to collect plants for the same reason.

Wild plants should not become the only source of nourishment. It is possible, however, to make them a frequent and interesting supplement to healthy eating when, for example, holidaying in the countryside. Such expeditions will provide you with fresh air and exercise and can be quite educational not only for you, but for the rest of the family as well.

NOTE: Some species mentioned in this book may be hard to find, and you may wish to grow them in your own garden. If seeds, tubers etc are hard to obtain, small specialist nurseries may be the answer. Some companies may even be able to import them for you.

PROTECTIVE AND EFFECTIVE SUBSTANCES IN WILD PLANTS

Vitamins

The substances most valuable to the human body contained in wild plants are vitamins. They are present in plants in small quantities and in variable amounts. A complete lack of vitamins in the diet eventually leads to avitominosis which can seriously endanger health.

Vitamin C (L-ascorbic acid) is most widespread in plants. The recommended daily dosage is 60 to 150 mg and is necessary to maintain normal bodily functions. It is important in the formation of connecting tissue, the healing of wounds and to combat infection. A daily dosage of about 100 mg helps to ward off diseases of the upper respiratory tract. Vitamin C also aids in the formation of blood, the absorption of iron and the well-being of the nervous system. Sufficient doses are important in convalescence, for small children, old people, in pregnancy and in stress situations. In particular, children need it in regular daily doses. Deficiency manifests itself in fatigue and irritation, bleeding gums and the reduced resistance of the body. It is not stored by the body as a reserve and thus it is necessary to receive it regularly. Vitamin C acquired from natural sources is more desirable than its manufactured equivalent.

Vitamin C degenerates in heat, in the air, in light and when in contact with metals. It is soluble in water and is therefore washed away by the prolonged soaking of plants in water. Interestingly, it is more stable in an acid environment; this is why salad dressings contain lemon juice or vinegar. Fresh plants contain the largest amounts of vitamin C. The highest vitamin C content occurs in rosehips (as much as 2000 mg in 100 g), buckthorn (350—1000 mg), black currants (as much as 400 mg) and citrus fruit (about 50 mg). A similarly high vitamin C content is present in chives, horseradish, nettle, woodland fruits, barberries and a number of other wild plants.

The vitamins of group B are also soluble in water. This group consists of several vitamins as detailed below.

Vitamin B$_1$ (aneurin, tiamin) protects the nervous system, greatly assists the functioning of the stomach and the absorption by the body of saccharides. It is present in hazelnuts, chestnuts, rosehips and in the largest quantities in cereals. It is destroyed by lengthy boiling. A higher intake is necessary in situations involving physical strain, mental stress, during pregnancy and by those who smoke or drink heavily.

Vitamin B$_2$ (riboflavin, lactoflavin) influences oxidoreductive processes and the growth and renewal of cells. It is a component of every living cell and can be found in rosehips, chives, leaf vegetables and animal products such as liver, milk and eggs. A lack of it leads to inflammations of mucous membranes and sore corners of mouth.

Vitamin B$_6$ (pyrydoxin, adermin) regulates the functioning of the nervous system and stimulates a good skin condition and digestion. It is found in strawberries, cherries, apples and nuts, and is particularly important after a course of antibiotics, for patients suffering from polyarthritis and for women who use hormonal contraceptives. A deficiency causes skin and nervous changes.

Vitamin PP (nicotinic acid, presently called niacin) regulates the function of the stomach and contributes to the transformation of substances during digestion. A lack of it leads to skin inflammations, diarrhoea and mental disorders. It is mostly found in animal products such as kidneys, liver and heart, but also occurs in the leaves of wild plants, rosehips, cereals, mushrooms and elsewhere.

Vitamin B$_3$ (pantothenic acid) plays an important role in maintaining proper functioning of the metabolism. It is usually present in the body in sufficient quantities and is found in beetroot, beans and fresh plants.

Folic acid is present above all in fresh green leaves, as well as liver, meat and eggs. It is important for the formation of blood, in particular of red blood cells. It also has an effect on the digestive system and on the healthy state of the mucous membrane in the mouth.

Vitamin D is made up of a number of substances. It is formed in the skin when sun's rays shine on it. It is contained in mushrooms, the leaves of green plants and in particular in cod liver oil. It assists the build up of calcium in the bones and protects against rickets.

Vitamin E (tocopherols) is formed by several chemically related substances and is found in plant oils, the seeds of rosehips, and the leaves of plants. It has a favourable effect on fertility, is soluble in fat and protects vitamin A and fats from oxidation.

Vitamin K (methylnaphtoquinone) aids the coagulation of blood, is soluble in fat and is present in chestnut leaves, the needles of coniferous trees, as well as in rosehips and strawberries.

Vitamin P (rutin, hesperidin, citrin) is a group of substances called at present flavonoides or bioflavonoides. These are 'free' or 'glycosidic' substances. Their range of activity is extensive. They normalize the permeability of the capillaries; they lessen their fragility, they increase the effectiveness of vitamin C and the secretion of gall. They have diuretic, anti-varicose and anti-infection effect. Some influence the coagulation of blood or reduce blood pressure. Rutin, which is present in the flowers of the elder, has an important role in reducing bleeding, hypertension, allergies and infections. Hesperidin, present in citrus fruit, has a similar effect. Vitamin P is also found in rue, rosehips, raspberries, berries of mountain ash, cranberries, bilberries etc.

Vitamin A (retinol) is present in plants in the form of carotenes, the provitamin A, and is formed in the body's intestinal wall from carotenes, which are present in mountain ash berries, rosehips, red currants, the fruit of the buckthorn, the leaves of nettles, sorrel and dandelion. They are sensitive to oxygen. Animal products, especially liver, are an important source of vitamin A. It is most needed in times of development and growth and when suffering from liver diseases. It is best absorbed in conjunction with fats, as it dissolves in them; this is why oil is added to salads. Vitamin A positively influences physical growth and the condition of the skin and mucous membranes. When it is lacking, the skin becomes rough, especially on the rear sides of the arms and calves and the vision is impaired in dim lighting.

Vitamin F is a dated term for a group of essential aliphatic acids (mainly linoleic and linolenic), all necessary for the proper functioning of the body. Aliphatic acids slow down the ageing of blood vessels. They are found in vegetable oils, for example in buckthorn. They belong to the B-complex group.

Saccharides
Saccharides, formerly called carbohydrates, are products of the primary metabolism of plants. They are an important source of energy present in plants as simple sugars (monosaccharides), oligosaccharides (combined from several simple sugars, for example sucrose) and polysaccharides (combined sugars). Glucose and fructose are simple sugars, can be easily digested and are soluble in water. Sucrose, on the other hand, must be broken down by the human body.

Polysaccharides are present in tubers and roots. They are insoluble and include starches, inulin, cellulose, hemicellulose and lignin. Cellulose together with hemicellulose and lignin form a coarse, fibrous material which helps prevent constipation and slows down the absorption of cholesterol. It is contained in cereals, vegetables, fruit and nettle leaves. Inulin is a well-known substance obtained from the roots of plants belonging to the family Compositae. It is easily digestible by those suffering from diabetes.

Polysaccharides also include pectins which are able to swell up greatly and form jelly. Therefore they regulate the digestive process and influence the functioning of the intestines. They are present in berries, apples, strawberries, citrus fruit, red currants and in other plants. Polysaccharides also include a mucus substance which protects the mucous membrane of the intestinal tract and the skin. It is contained in plantain, coltsfoot, lime etc.

Fats
Fats are a concentrated source of energy. In plants they occur usually in the form of oils. They often contain unsaturated aliphatic acids which aid the degenerative processes in blood vessels. They are present in hazelnuts, the seeds of the red elder, the fruit of the buckthorn, etc. Oils and fats also contain many other important substances, such as provitamin A, tocopherol (vitamin E) and others.

Proteins and nitrogenous substances
Proteins, containing nitrogen, are present in every living tissue and belong to the basic nutrients. The main source of proteins are animal products but they can be also found in nuts, nettles, garlic, soya, peas etc. Nitrogen can also be found in plants as a metabolic by-product in the form of nitrates. In large concentrations in foodstuffs nitrates have a harmful effect on human beings, especially young children. They develop in excessive quantities when there is a lack of light and an excess of nitrogen in the soil. This occurs more frequently in the root system and the leaf veins than in the fruit or in young, unripe plants.

Tannins
Tannins are natural nitrogen-free substances with a variable effect. They are mainly present in the bark, roots and also in leaves and fruits. They inhibit bleeding, check diarrhoea and sweating. The have a styptic, antibacterial, antiviral and anti-inflammatory effect. They are abundantly present in blackthorn, wild pear, cornelian cherries, mountain ash berries, bilberries, raspberries, hyssop, sage, common thyme and many other plants.

Alkaloids
Alkaloids develop during the breakdown of proteins. They are natural nitrogen-bearing substances having a strong effect on the human

10

body. Their names are usually derived from the generic name of the plant from which they have been isolated and are usually poisonous. They are found for example in the wood of the barberry, though not in the fruit, a negligible amount in yarrow and other plants. They are used in an isolated form in medicinal preparations.

Glycosides
Glycosides are substances containing sugars but they are mostly active through their non-sugar elements and are the 'building blocks' of plants. They are contained in the cell sap. Some are poisonous, for example the glycosides of hydrogen cyanide found in cherry stones, Morello cherries, bitter almonds and elsewhere. They have a variable effect on the human organism. Phenol glycosides, for example arbutin in cranberries, have a disinfective effect on the urinary tract. Coumarine glycosides in sweet woodruff and other plants have spasmolytic and diuretic effects and a calming influence on the central nervous system. Flavone glycosides can be found in almost all plants and they increase the resistance of the capillaries. Glycosides contained in red elder flowers assist perspiration.

Saponins
Saponins are froth-forming substances related to glycosides. They promote digestion, loosen phlegm and have an anti-inflammatory effect. They are contained in nettles, spinach, liquorice and birch.

Essential oils
Essential oils, also called volatile oils, are usually liquid mixtures of volatile, often aromatic substances. Most frequently they have an oily consistency. They are stored in specialized cells, in glands and in certain tissues of the plants. Their content fluctuates according to the developmental stage of the plant and also according to the time of day. They are used in food, cosmetics and pharmaceutical industries. They cure inflammations of the upper respiratory system (wild thyme, garden thyme) and of the digestive tract (caraway, mint, garden thyme), influence the secretion of urine (juniper berries) and have an antiseptic effect on the urinary tract (horse-radish), on intestinal parasites (garlic, fat hen). They also have a calming effect (balm, rosemary, lavender), disinfect the mouth (sage, basil) etc. The essential oils of plants used as herbs also belong to this group (caraway, mustard, garden thyme, sweet flag, oregano). Essential oils can be found in almost all fruit and plants, however the greatest concentrations are to be found in plants belonging to the mint, carrot and borage families and in citrus fruits.

Organic acids

Organic acids have a sour taste and are mainly present in fruit. They speed up peristalsis of the digestive tract and promote the formation of urine. Best known of these are the malic, citric and tartaric acid. If taken in large quantities, oxalic acid is harmful to human health since it removes calcium from the body. Plants containing oxalic acid such as sorrel, wood sorrel, spinach, and in small amounts currants and gooseberries, should not be consumed in large quantities and food prepared from them should be supplemented with milk. Salicylic acid present in raspberries has a fever-reducing effect. Benzoic acid in cranberries and cowberries stabilises the products made from these fruits.

Phytoncides

This is a group of substances with a varied chemical composition. Phytoncides limit the development of or kill some microorganisms, thereby protecting us from infection and helping to heal wounds. They are present in almost all plants which use them as a protective barrier against disease. They are found in yarrow, garlic, horseradish, chives, nettles, wild thyme, garden thyme, lavender, cranberries, black currants and in a number of other plants.

Enzymes (ferments)

Enzymes are present in every living cell and are closely connected with vitamins. They assist the plants' effect on the human organism and take part in all live and decomposing processes of a cell. They influence the digestion and the transformation of complex substances into simple ones and vice versa. They are destroyed by boiling and too long storage and therefore plants should ideally be consumed in their fresh state.

Bitter principles

These are natural substances with a complex chemical composition and a bitter taste. They assist the secretion of digestive juices, and the activity of the gall-bladder and liver. They have anti-convulsive, anti-inflammatory and styptic effects, and improve the appetite, digestion and intestinal peristalsis. Bitter principles are present in stemless thistle, yarrow, hop, dandelions and many plants from the mint family.

Minerals

The most important of these are potassium, sodium, calcium, magnesium, phosphorus, sulphur, copper, iron, manganese, zinc and silicon.

In plants they are present as the salts of various substances. Some of them, i.e. trace elements and micro-elements, are needed in gramme dosages, others only in fractions of milligrammes.

Potassium has a diuretic effect; it influences the nervous and muscular activity of the cardiac muscle, and also has a beneficial influence on the skin. It is present in stone fruit, horse-radish, garlic, colt's-foot and the leaves of various members of the birch family.

Sodium helps retain liquids in the body; it influences digestion and when taken in larger quantities, it increases blood pressure. We usually acquire it from kitchen salt. In small quantities it is present in dandelion leaves, in chicory and in the smallest quantities in fruit.

Calcium is necessary for the building of bones, teeth and body tissue. It influences the coagulation of blood; it has a favourable effect on the nerves and heart. Berries, such as currants and gooseberries, contain the largest amount. It is also in hazelnuts, strawberries, cherries etc. It is especially necessary for growing children.

Magnesium improves the blood supply to the heart; it influences the formation of bones, the metabolism and the distribution of calcium in the body. Shortage of magnesium in the body manifests itself in irritable behaviour. In commercially produced foodstuffs its presence is reduced but it is found in green leaves, blackberries, apples, strawberries and some other plants.

Phosphorus is contained in the cell nucleus. It has a decisive effect on the metabolism of saccharides, fats and proteins and on the building of bones and teeth. It is present in hazelnuts, garlic and various berries.

Other elements, most importantly those which follow, are needed by the body in smaller quantities.

Iron, a component of pigment occurring in the blood, participates in oxidation processes and as an element in enzymes plays a part in the formation of blood. It is found in cherries, Morello cherries, strawberries, bilberries, cranberries, quinces, nettles and other plants.

Sulphur plays a role in the building of proteins and is important in the functioning of the liver. It is contained in garlic, brassicas, nuts and other plants.

Copper is important in the formation of blood, enzymatic activity and the nervous system. The largest amount of copper is present in the liver. Plants which contain copper include blackberries, ornamental cherries, quinces, chestnuts, Morello cherries, gooseberries, etc.

Manganese speeds up oxidation processes in the body. It influences growth, in particular the normal development of limbs. It is present in strawberries, bilberries, blackberries, cranberries, in cereals and in tea.

Zinc plays a part in the metabolism of saccharides and proteins. Any shortage causes a lessening in the sense of taste and smell, the slow healing of wounds and the slowing down of sexual development. It is mostly found in animal products. In plants, the highest levels of zinc are found in the leaves of ribwort and in apples.

Silicon occurs in plants quite frequently. It is necessary for strong bones, healthy hair and nails.

Other trace elements needed in small quantities include aluminium (in rhubarb, spinach), iodine (in lettuce, cabbage), chlorine (in beetroot), boron (more in fruit, less in vegetables), molybdenum (in peas), cobalt (in beetroot) and nickel (in leaf vegetables). In larger quantities heavy metals, such as lead, cadmium, mercury and others are harmful. They penetrate fruit, vegetables and herbs through the environment, mainly from car exhaust fumes. For this reason wild plants growing in close proximity to busy roads should not be collected.

IMPORTANT THINGS TO REMEMBER
WHEN COLLECTING WILD PLANTS

Only well-known plants should be collected. You will be able to acquaint yourself with the most frequently used wild species by studying the illustrations found further on in the book. Plants should be gathered only in such quantities which can be consumed straight away. Species which can be easily confused with poisonous plants (especially some members of the carrot family) must be collected with proper care and must never be collected by children. It is probably not a good idea to allow children to pick wild plants anyway, to be on the safe side.

Only healthy, apparently undamaged plants should be picked. Excessively lush growths from places with a high nitrogen content should be avoided; they could contain an unduly high amount of unwanted nitrates. Neither should plants be collected from the vicinity of rubbish dumps, dung-hills, or dusty and busy roads because of the danger of contamination by exhaust fumes or infectious germs. Near roads and highways plants should be collected at least 100 metres from the edge of the nearest thoroughfare. Collection should also be avoided alongside railways, industrial sites and agricultural complexes with dense animal populations. Similarly, areas close to chemically treated fields and meadows and areas with a high chemical fall-out should be avoided.

Protected plants or those growing in conservation areas should never be picked. After all, these days it is the duty of every individual to protect the countryside.

When collecting plants it should be borne in mind that the point of the exercise is not to wipe out a species completely. Therefore, sufficient plants need to be left behind in order to allow a particular colony to regenerate for future collectors. Care should be taken to leave behind ripe fruit or seeds. In the case of perennial plants the underground parts, the roots and shoots should be saved if they are not being collected. However, even then several mature plants should be left untouched on every site. Along the same lines, if you come across a site which has obviously been recently harvested, you should not then proceed to divest it completely of all plants, rather it should be left alone.

Wild plants are collected from sites where they can be found in abundance. They are collected with the utmost care (i. e. the stems are not pulled out along with the roots), so that they are preserved for the future in at least their present numbers. The locations for collection need to be alternated regularly.

When collecting plants, it is best to use gloves and various tools, such as secateurs, knives or special trowels. They make work simpler, easier and cleaner.

The gathered plants are placed loosely in baskets, without being closely packed. They must be treated gently, otherwise an unwanted fermentation can take place. The sturdier parts of plants, shoots and tough stems can be carried in bags and sacks.

Fresh plants should not be stored for a long time but consumed the same day. First, they must be sorted and washed, but without an unnecessarily long soaking in order to avoid losing valuable substances such as vitamin C. For cutting and grating only stainless steel or plastic knives should be used. If you do not wish to use them immediately, the best way to preserve plants is by freezing or drying. They can be dried in the shade and in a draft or by artificial heat at a temperature of about 40 °C. Fruits can be dried in the sun. Dried plants are usually stored in paper bags or airtight glass or tin containers. Plastic containers should be avoided. Plants should be kept in a dry, cold (to 15 °C) and dark place. They must be clearly labelled. More detailed instructions regarding plant preparation are given individually.

HOW, WHAT AND WHEN TO COLLECT

You cannot collect plants at just any time. It depends on when the plant or some of its parts contain the maximum concentration of beneficial substances. This is because biochemical reactions which change the composition of the plants are constantly taking place. It is therefore necessary to be aware of the substances present in each part of the plant to be collected and also the conditions which may affect them.

Flower (*flos*)

Flowers are the reproductive organs of plants. They grow singly as for example in roses or violets, in groups like the hawthorn, yarrow or colt's-foot. They should be collected at midday in dry weather. Late afternoon or a damp morning are not really suitable times. Flowers should be picked before full bloom, before they start to fall or the fruit begins to form. Some flowers, such as hawthorn, are picked when the plant starts to flower, others, such as the daisy, are collected in bud form. Flowers are picked individually or the whole inflorescences, such as those of the yarrow, are cut with scissors or a knife. Individual petals can be subsequently picked from large flowers like the pot marigold. Once picked, flowers are sensitive to being overheated. Bruised and damaged flowers can change colour and the substances they contain become worthless. They should never be placed in plastic bags as this causes them to sweat.

Fruit (*fructus*)

Fruits develop from pollinated flowers and contain one or more seeds. The pulpy casing, such as in the apple, can be eaten or alternatively the seeds, such as in the case of the hazelnut. Fruits and seeds are usually gathered when fully ripe or just before.

Bud (*gemma*)

Buds are globe-shaped or pointed embryos of branches with leaves or flowers attached. They should be collected when they begin to open and then placed in a basket so that they do not become overheated.

Leaf (*folium*)

Leaves together with roots absorb nutrients from the surrounding environment. They are most often collected before the plant begins to flower for it is at this stage that they contain the largest amounts of their effective substances. The young, healthy and juicy leaves are selected, never the old leaves close to the ground or those covered with mud. During collection it is necessary to take care not to deprive the plant of its entire assimilative surface. Leaves should be picked carefully and not be closely packed, as they are sensitive to overheating. When treated roughly, the green chlorophyll decomposes and the leaves turn brown.

16

Tops (*herba*)

Tops are that part of the plant which grows above the ground, namely the stalk with its leaves and possibly with flowers and fruits. It should be cut off with scissors or with a sharp knife, not pulled or broken off as it is easy to pull a plant out at the roots thus destroying it. Plants which grow close to the ground or have a tendency to be flat are particularly vulnerable in this way. The aerial parts should be harvested when young at the time of or shortly before flowering. Later on the fibrous part increases, they become tough, and their valuable substances decrease. In tall plants only the top 15—20 cm should be cut. Lower parts tend to be woody, tough and unsuitable for use. All parts of plants, in particular stems with leaves, should have their natural colour. Plants with a dark blue-green colouring which indicates an excess of nitrogen or conversely with a light green to yellow hue or variegated colouring should be avoided. Of course all plants should be thoroughly washed before use. The aerial parts have fewer beneficial qualities than the leaves and flowers but are easier to gather.

Root (*radix*)

The root is the underground organ of a plant supplying it with soluble nutrients, and often containing substances of great medicinal value. It differs from the rhizome and underground runners by the absence of leaves or leaf scales. Roots should be gathered during the period of vegetative dormancy, that is in autumn just before the plant stops growing in October or November or early in spring when the plant is just beginning to develop. At this time they contain the greatest amounts of valuable substances. Later in spring they become woody and lose their flavour. They can be most easily pulled out when the soil is moist. The roots of perennials should be harvested in the second or third year of growth. Damaged, rotten or deformed roots should not be collected. Small roots, shoots and tubers must be left in the soil in order to guarantee that the plant will develop during the following season. Before preparation the roots must be thoroughly free of dirt and soil. They should not be scrubbed with a brush as this can destroy surface cells.

POISONOUS PLANTS — BEWARE!

Poisoning by plants does not occur very frequently and when it does it is usually a matter of a child eating the fruits, seeds or flowers of the plant.

Poisonous plants grow in exactly the same conditions as any other plant. They can be found in fields, meadows and other places but many grow in parks or even at home in a flowerpot. The poisonous substances they contain can be distributed throughout the plant in a number of different ways; either the whole plant is poisonous or the toxic substances may be concentrated in one of its parts, most frequently in the fruit. These plants do not contain only one poisonous substance but a single plant species can contain a number of them. Usually these are alkaloids, glycosides, saponins and some volatile oils. Plants which are not well known should *never* be picked! Some of the more easily mistaken and most dangerous poisonous plants are described below.

Lily of the valley (*Convallaria majalis*) contains glycosides which have a harmful effect on the heart. Its leaves can be mistaken for the leaves of wild garlic, the latter, however, do have a very strong garlic odour. Similarly the fruits of lily of the valley, that is its red berries, can be mistaken for other woodland fruits. Although the leaves of lily of the valley are different from the leaves of cranberry and blueberry, poisoning from its fruit still does occur, causing stupor, sickness and strong urination. The leaves of the very poisonous **false helleborine** (*Veratrum album*) are also similar to those of wild garlic, however as before one should be aware that this poisonous plant does not smell of garlic.

The worst problems of mistaken identity are caused by the medicinally and economically important carrot family. This consists of about 1,000 similar species in 140 genera. These include plants with a carrot-like white root, a hollow stem, variously shaped leaves forming a basal rosette, with an umbrella-shaped cluster of whitish flowers and egg-shaped fruits which split into two small achenes. Many of them are commonly known, for example caraway, fennel, parsley and carrots. Poisoning by the members of the carrot family is quite frequent but luckily it is not very serious. Once again, children should not collect these plants, especially their fruits. Certain members of the carrot family could be confused with **hemlock** (*Conium maculatum*). This grows to a height of 2 metres and smells of rotten meat, especially when it starts to fade. It can be found along fences, in thickets and in damp places, never forming continuous growths, however. **Rough chervil** (*Chaerophyllum temulum*) is another dangerous member of the carrot family. It resembles parsley and its fruits are reminiscent of caraway seeds.

Some poisonous berries may look edible because of their attractive appearance, such as those of **mezereon** (*Daphne mezereum*), which look rather like red currants. Similarly attractive are the fruits of the very dangerous **deadly nightshade** (*Atropa bella-donna*) — relatively large red berries enclosed in a large calyx or outer casing of leaves.

Their taste is repulsive but they can be mistakenly collected when picking edible woodland berries in forest clearings and glades, where the deadly nightshade also grows. Some other members of the nightshade family also have dangerous fruit, which can be mistaken for edible woodland berries, such as those of the woody nightshade (*Solanum dulcamara*), a climbing semi-shrub with dark red oval berries to be found in thickets in damp places. The globe-shaped berries of **black nightshade** (*Solanum nigra*), measuring almost 1 cm in diameter, can be mistaken for black currants or bilberries. This plant grows on fallow and waste land and is considerably different from those species yielding edible fruit. The poisonous fruits of **herb paris** (*Paris quadrifolia*) can be mistaken for bilberries. They grow singly on an erect stem surrounded by four characteristically large leaves and are bluish-black berries similar in size to wild cherries. The overall appearance of the plant, however, is completely different from that of a bilberry.

Slight poisoning can be also caused by the fruit of some members of the genus *Lonicera,* e.g. **fly honeysuckle** (*Lonicera xylosteum*) whose light red berries are transparent and grow in pairs on a stalk. Low shrubs of **black honeysuckle** (*Lonicera nigra*) often grow at the foot of the mountains amongst bilberry shrubs.

Poisonous plants do not occur in small numbers. However, with some care the danger of being poisoned by such plants is quite rare. If you want to get to know them better, it is important to make a thorough study of the subject.

WILD PLANTS AS FOOD

Delicious food can be prepared from wild plants using similar techniques as in the preparation of cultivated plants. Leafy parts should be prepared in the same way as ordinary lettuce, spinach, beet, cabbage, white cabbage or leafy vegetables. Roots and tubers should be treated like root vegetables or potatoes. Flowers may be used in the preparation of teas, syrups, soft drinks and wines or they can be added to salads or dipped in batter and fried. If possible, wild fruit should be consumed fresh or it may be made into soups, sauces, juices, syrups, wines and liqueurs. Wild fruit can also be bottled, dried or frozen.

The length of cooking time for a wild plant depends on its stage of development. For young leaves and tops usually 15 minutes is sufficient, for older leaves and tops 20 to 30 minutes may be necessary. Before cooking it is advisable to test the length of cooking time on a small quantity of plants. Young plants are preferable as ageing increases the fibrous content and some plants do lose their pleasant taste.

Some wild plants have a specific flavour which does not appeal to everybody. For example goutweed smells of carrots, similarly hogweed might not be appreciated by everybody. In order to tone down the flavours, therefore, plants should first be scalded with boiling water and then prepared. It is best to mix several species together, especially if you are making a dish using leaves. Wild plants can also be used to complement cultivated vegetables and meat courses. Most people seem to like nettles, dock and also orache and goose-foot mixed together with spinach, beet or other aromatic herbs.

Wild plants can also be employed in a weight-reducing diet. According to analysis their energy value is similar to the green parts of spinach or cabbage and varies from 80 to 200 kJ in 100 g of matter and in their underground parts from 150 to 550 kJ. Only hazelnuts, beechnuts, chestnuts and pinenuts, containing a considerable amount of vegetable oils or starches, have a higher energy value, rising to about 2,000 kJ in 100 g.

It is interesting to compare the vitamin C content of some wild plants and vegetables. For example, spinach contains about 50 mg of vitamin C in 100 g, nettles as much as 150 mg, dock 77 mg, orache 150 mg, lady's mantle 216 mg, white goosefoot as much as 245 mg. These plants are thus well worth using in the kitchen, especially in spring when the concentration of vitamin C is high. They also contain many other valuable substances.

When comparing the vitamin C content in wild and cultivated fruits, it becomes evident that wild apples have 15 to 30 mg of vitamin C whilst cultivated species usually 4 to 10 mg in 100 g of pulp. A large difference is also apparent in wild cherries, which contain about 30 mg of vitamin C in 100 g of pulp, whilst the cultivated varieties have only 10 mg at the most.

Similarly, wild plants used in the preparation of teas usually have a high vitamin C content. The most common species, such as the leaves of the Blackberry and the Raspberry, have about 40 to 50 mg in 100 g, strawberry leaves about 200 mg. A particularly high content is present in rosehips, rowanberries and buckthorn.

Because of the high vitamin C content it is quite often sufficient to consume only 100 to 200 mg of wild plants even taking into account the loss through heat preparation and without even considering the other valuable substances contained within them.

TABLE OF SELECTED WILD PLANTS

plant	collected part	month of collection	use in kitchen	medicinal effects
Achillea millefolium Yarrow	leaf	IV.—V.	in soups, sauces, omelets	improves digestion and appetite
	flower	V.—IX.	to season dishes	
Acorus calamus Sweet-flag	rhizome	III.—IV. IX.—XI.	to spice liqueurs, sauces, soups, sweetmeats, compotes, brandy, tea, vegetables	improves digestion and appetite
	leaf	III.—IV.	in salads	
Aegopodium podagraria Goutweed	leaf	IV.—XI.	in soups, salads	source of vitamins
Alchemilla xanthochlora Lady's Mantle	leaf	V.—IX.	in soups, spinach, vegetable dishes	assists digestion, diuretic properties
Alliaria petiolata Garlic Mustard	leaf	IV.—XI.	in soups, sauces, spreads, stuffings, vegetable salads, forcemeat, lamb	antispasmodic and disinfectant effect on digestive tract
	seeds	IV.—XI.	to season dishes	
Allium schoenoprasum Chives	leaf	IV.—V.	in soups, sauces, egg dishes, salads, mayonnaise, spreads, herb butters	improves digestion, appetite, lowers blood pressure
Allium ursinum Wild Garlic	tops	IV.—V.	in salads, vegetables, pulses, sauces, stuffings, minced meats, mayonnaise, spreads, with fish, poultry, in herb butters	antispasmodic and disinfective effect on digestive tract
	bulb	IX.—X.		
Allium victoriale Long-rooted Garlic	leaf	IV.—VI.	in soups, sauces, mayonnaise, salads, spreads, on grilled meats, with lamb, pork, fish	improves digestion and appetite, diuretic properties
	bulb	IX.—X.		
Amelanchier ovalis Service-berry	fruit	IX.—X.	for jams, jellies, marmalades, juices, wines, tea	against common colds, to check hypovitaminosis
Angelica archangelica Angelica	leaf, stem	V.—VI.	in salads, soups, sauces, vegetables	improves digestion, diuretic, disinfectant, calming effects
	fruit root	IX. III.—IV., IX.—XI.	to season dishes	
Arctium lappa Great Burdock	root	III.—V., IX.—XI.	in salads, vegetable side dish	perspiratory, diuretic, bactericidal effects, to check digestive disorders
	leaf	III.—XI.	in salads, soups	

plant	collected part	month of collection	use in kitchen	medicinal effects
Armocaria rusticana Horse-radish	root	III.—V., X.—XI.	freshly grated to boiled meats, eggs, smoked meats, fish, vegetables, in soups, sauces, spreads	improves digestion, bactericidal effects
	leaf	III.—XI.	in soups, to spice pickled vegetables	
Atriplex hortensis Garden Orache	leaf	IV.—V.	as substitution for spinach, in soups, with vegetables, in stuffings, forcemeat, egg dishes	assists evacuation of bowels, production of blood
Bellis perennis Daisy	leaf and buds	III.—V.	in salads, herb butter, soups, sauces, stuffings, spreads, omelets	anti-inflammatory effects, for treating diseases of respiratory tract, source of vitamin C
	flower	III.—XII.	for syrup	
Berberis vulgaris Barberry	fruit	IX.—X.	for juices, syrups, wines, liqueurs, compotes, jam, tea; can be frozen, dried; dried in sauces with game, soups and with grilled meats	influences activity of stomach and bowels, improves appetite, source of vitamins
Betula pendula Silver Birch	juice	III.—IV.	for syrup, 'Birch Champagne'	antispasmodic and diuretic effects
Borago officinalis Borage	leaf	IV.—X.	in salads, ragout, cold sauces and soups, spreads, mayonnaise, forcemeat, cold drinks, as fillings for pies and ravioli	diuretic, disinfective, calming effects, ingredient of spring cures
	flower	V.—IX.	in soups, desserts, candied	
Calendula officinalis Pot Marigold	flower	V.—X.	seasoning (soups, sauces), food colouring	diuretic, perspiratory, antiinflammatory, antispasmodic effects
	leaf	VI.—IX.	in soups, salads	
Campanula rapunculus Rampion	root	III.—IV.	in salads, soups, vegetable side dishes, in vegetable mixtures	to check diabetes, source of vitamins
Carlina acaulis Stemless Thistle	flower	VII.—IX.	raw or cooked as artichokes	bactericidal, diuretic effects
Carum carvi Caraway	fruit	VII.—VIII.	to season bread, pastries, meat, soups, cheeses, vegetables, liqueurs	improves digestion of heavy food, appetite, carminative effects
	leaf	IV.—V.	in herb soups, salads, spreads	

plant	collected part	month of collection	use in kitchen	medicinal effects
Castanea sativa Sweet Chestnut	fruit	X.—XI.	in soups, purée, desserts, meat stuffings	for high blood pressure and kidney diseases
Chaerophyllum bulbosum Tuberous-rooted Chervil	root	III.—IV., X.—XI.	in salads, boiled like potatoes or root vegetables	improves digestion and appetite, source of vitamins
	leaf	III.—XI.	in salads, soups	
Chenopodium album Fat Hen	leaf	IV.—XI.	in soups, stuffings, minced meats, potato dishes, as substitution for spinach	improves evacuation of bowels and blood production
Cornus mas Cornelian Cherry	fruit	IX.	for juices, wines, syrups, liqueurs, jams, compotes, vitaminized teas	disorders of digestive tract, diuretic effects, induces production of bile, source of vitamins
Corylus avellana Hazel	seeds	IX.—X.	in desserts, chocolate, puddings, ice cream, fruit salads, meat stuffings	high content of nutritious substances, grated with honey as cough cure
Crataegus laevigata Midland Hawthorn	buds	IV.—V.	in salads, soft cheese spreads	with heart and blood circulation diseases
	fruit	X.—XI.	for syrups, teas	
Cydonia oblonga Quince	fruit	X.	for cider, compotes, jelly, in meat dishes, can be dried	disorders of digestive tract
Cyperus esculentus Chufa	tubers	X.	in sweetmeats, boiled as vegetables, raw as almonds, roasted as peanuts	high content of nutritious substances
Epilobium angustifolium Rosebay Willowherb	leaf	IV.—X.	for tea	calming effects
	rootstock	III.—VI., X.—XI.	for salads, compote	
Fagus sylvatica Beech	fruit	X.—XI.	dried or roasted for direct use, ground in sweetmeats	high content of nutritious substances
Fragaria moschata Hautbois Strawberry	fruit	VI.—VII.	for jams, compotes, syrups, in desserts, soups	disorders of digestive tract diuretic effects
	leaf	V.—VII.	for tea	
Fragaria vesca Wood Strawberry	fruit	VI.—VII.	for compotes, marmalades, juices, syrups, wines, filling for desserts	improves digestion, diuretic effects
	leaf	V.—VII.	in soups, for tea	
Fragaria viridis Wild Strawberry	fruit	VI.—VII.	for compotes, marmalades, syrups, wines, filling for desserts	improves digestion, diuretic effects
	leaf	V.—VII.	in soups, for tea	
Galium odoratum Sweet Woodruff	tops	V.—VI.	to aromatize wine, milk, puddings, ciders, fruit soups, sauces, drinks	overall calming effect
Geum urbanum Wood Avens	rhizome	III.—IV., XI.	as spice (to replace cloves and cinnamon)	disorders in digestion, improves appetite
	tops	III.—IV.	in herb soups and sauces	

plant	collected part	month of collection	use in kitchen	medicinal effects
Glechoma hederacea Ground-ivy	leaf	IV.—V.	in vegetable stews, meats, soups, salads, spreads	improves digestion and appetite
Glyceria fluitans Floating Sweetgrass	fruit	VIII.—IX.	to thicken soups, in purée	high content of nutritious substances
Grossularia uva-crispa Gooseberry	fruit	VI.—VII.	for marmalades, jellies, compotes, juices, cold soups and sauces	diuretic, slight laxative effects
Heracleum sphondylium Cow Parsnip	leaf	IV.—IX.	as spinach, in soups	improves digestion, calming effects
Hippophaë rhamnoides Sea Buckthorn	fruit	VIII.—IX.	for juices, syrups, jams, marmalades, compotes, sauce to accompany game and grilled meats	source of vitamins during infectious diseases, hypovitaminosis, in convalescence
Humulus lupulus Hop	shoots	III.—IV.	for salads, soups, as a side dish	calming, diuretic effects, improves digestion
Hyssopus officionalis Hyssop	leaf	VI.—IX.	to season salads, minced meats, sauces, soups, game, chicken	improves digestion
Juniperus communis Juniper	fruit	X.—XI.	to season game, lamb, sauerkraut, sauces, poultry	assists digestion of heavy food
Malus Apple	fruit	VII.—IX.	for ciders, juices, wines, syrups, can be baked and dried	diuretic, calming effects
Melissa officinalis Balm	leaf	VI.—VII.	to season food, wines, liqueurs, vinegars, for tea	digestive disorders, calming effects
Mespilus germanica Medlar	fruit	X.—XI.	for ciders, marmalades, syrups, wines	digestive disorders
Morus alba White Mulberry	fruit	VII.—VIII.	for ciders, wines, compotes, drinks from fresh juice, syrups	improves digestion, relieves sore throat, diuretic effects
Morus nigra Black Mulberry	fruit	VII.—IX.	for ciders, preserves, wines, compotes	improves digestion, relieves sore throat, dietetic effects, in diseases of pancreas
	leaf	VI.—VIII.	for tea	
Origanum vulgare Marjoram	tops	VI.—VIII.	to season forcemeats, sauces, pizzas, risittos, vegetable dishes, cheeses	improves digestion and appetite

24

plant	collected part	month of collection	use in kitchen	medicinal effects
Oxalis acetosella Wood-sorrel	leaf	IV.—V., X.—XI.	in vegetable soups, sauces, mayonnaise, yoghurt salads, drinks	digestive disorders, diuretic effects
Pimpinella major Greater Burnet-saxifrage	leaf	IV.—V.	in soups, sauces, mayonnaise, spreads, stuffings, salads, vegetables	digestive disorders, in diseases of respiratory tract
	root	III.—V., IX.	for tea	
Pimpinella saxifraga Burnet-saxifrage	leaf	V.—VI.	in soups, mayonnaise, herb butters, spreads, salads, cream sauces, with meat	digestive disorders, improves appetite, in diseases of respiratory tract
	root	III.—V., IX.	for tea	
Pinus pinea Umbrella Pine	seeds	X.—XI.	in meat and vegetable dishes, sweetmeats	diuretic effects, high content of nutritious substances, source of vitamins
	needles	IV.—V.	for vitaminized drinks	
Plantago lanceolata Ribwort Plantain	leaf	V.—VIII.	in soups, sauces, salads, for syrups	digestion disorders, diseases of respiratory tract
Polygonum hydropiper Water-pepper	tops	VII.—IX.	to season salads, spreads, soups, sauces, meat dishes, stuffings	digestion disorders, diuretic effects
Portulaca oleracea Purslane	tops	V.—IX.	in cucumber, tomato, lettuce salads, soups, sauces, mayonnaise, spreads	diuretic and calming effects
Prunus avium Wild Cherry	fruit	VI.—VII.	for ciders, wines, brandy, jams, compotes, fillings for desserts, drying	promotes production of blood, building of bones, teeth, diuretic effects
Prunus cerasifera Cherry Plum	fruit	IX.—X.	for spreads, sauces to grilled meats, wine, tea	in diseases of respiratory tract, improves digestion
Prunus cerasus Sour Cherry	fruit	VII.—VIII.	for syrups, drinks, jams, compotes, soups, fillings for desserts	digestion disorders, diuretic effects, to check anaemia
	leaf	VII.—XI.	to pickle gherkins and cabbage	
	fruit stalks	VII.—VIII.	for tea	
Prunus insititia Bullace	fruit	XI.	for compotes, marmalades, wines, fruit sauces, in desserts, savoury and meat dishes	in diseases of blood circulation, diuretic effects
Prunus spinosa Sloe	flower	III.—IV.	for teas and syrups	improves digestion, slightly laxative, anti-inflammatory effects, in colds, digestion disorders, diarrhoea, diuretic effects
	fruit	X.—XI.	for compotes, wines, vinegars, liqueurs, syrups, teas	

25

plant	collected part	month of collection	use in kitchen	medicinal effects
Pulmonaria officinalis Lungwort	leaf	III.—V.	in soups, spreads, stuffings, forcemeats, in salads, teas	improves digestion, diuretic effects, in diseases of respiratory tract
Pyrus Pear	fruit	X.—XI.	for vinegars, wines, in marmalades, ciders, drying	improves digestion, in blood circulation and kidney diseases
Ribes nigrum Black Currant	fruit	VI.—VII.	for jams, jellies, juices, marmalades, compotes, liqueurs, in soups, sauces, desserts	diuretic effects, source of vitamins, assists digestion, in diseases of respiratory tract
	leaf	V.—VIII.	to spice pickled gherkins and cabbage	
Rosa canina Dog Rose	fruit	IX.—X.	for preserves, wines, ketchups, soups, sauces with game, tea	improves digestion, production of blood, source of vitamins, diuretic effects
	flower	V.—VI.	for syrups, preserves, wines	
Rosa rugosa Japanese Rose	fruit	VIII.—IX.	for preserves, pastes, jellies, sweetmeats, teas	improves digestion, resistance of organism to diseases
	flower	V.—IX.	for wines, syrups, preserves, teas, in honey	
Rosa villosa Soft-leaved Rose	fruit	VIII.—IX.	for ketchups, marmalades, pastes soups, sauces with game, juices, syrups, teas, in honey	improves resistance of organism
	flower	V.—VI.	for wines, syrups	
Rubus fruticosus Blackberry	fruit	VIII.—IX.	for juices, soups, compotes, syrups, wines, liqueurs, fillings for desserts	improves digestion, calming effects
	leaf	VI.—VIII.	for tea	
Rubus idaeus Raspberry	fruit	VII.—IX.	for soups, salads, compotes, jams, fillings for desserts, syrups, juices, wines, liqueurs	improves digestion, diuretic effects
	leaf	V.—VIII.	for tea	
Rumex acetosa Common Sorrel	leaf	IV.—V.	as substitution for spinach, in salads, soups, sauces, mayonnaise, spreads, on grilled meats	assists digestion, production of blood, diuretic effects
Rumex acetosella Sheep's Sorrel	leaf	IV.—V.	as substitution for spinach, in soups, sauces, salads, mayonnaise, spreads, on grilled meats	assists digestion, production of blood, diuretic effects
Salvia officinalis Sage	leaf	IV.—VII.	to season lamb, pork, fish, tripe dishes, stuffings, pates, forcemeats, herb butters	in digestion disorders, calming effects
Salvia sclarea Clary	leaf	VI.	to spice wines, drinks, fruit soups, compotes, puddings, vinegar, vegetables	in digestive disorders, calming effects
Sambucus nigra Elder	fruit	VIII.—IX.	in jams, compotes, juices, wines, soups, syrups, sauces, liqueurs, wines, filling for desserts	diuretic, perspiratory, anti-inflammatory effects, in diseases of respiratory tract
	flower	V.—VII.	for wines, lemonades, drinks, syrups, teas	

plant	collected part	month of collection	use in kitchen	medicinal effects
Satureja montana Winter Savory	tops	VII.—IX.	to season poultry, game, fish, cheeses, pulses, stuffings, minced meats, smoked meats, suerkraut	improves digestion, appetite, against flatulence
Sempervivum tectorum Common Houseleek	leaf	IV.—XI.	for salads, vitaminized drinks	improves digestion and appetite, in diseases of respiratory tract
Sorbus aria Common Whitebeam	fruit	VIII.—IX.	for wines, compotes, teas	diuretic, anti-inflammatory effects, digestive disorders
Sorbus aucuparia Rowan	fruit	IX.	for compotes, syrups, ciders, liqueurs, jams, teas	laxative, diuretic effects, decreases blood pressure, source of vitamins
Sorbus aucuparia ssp. *moravica* Rowan	fruit	VIII.—IX.	for juices, syrups, compotes, preserves, liqueurs, wines, vinegars, brandy, teas	anti-inflammatory, diuretic effects, promotes secretion of bile, source of vitamins
Sorbus domestica Service-tree	fruit	IX.	for marmalades, wines, distilled beverages	in indigestion, source of vitamins
Sorbus torminalis Wild Service-tree	fruit	IX.—X.	in jams, marmalades, for liqueurs	source of vitamins
Stellaria media Common Chickweed	tops		in salads, in soups	source of vitamins, diuretic effects
Taraxacum officinale Dandelion	root	IV.—V.	in salads	improves digestion, dietetic, diuretic effects, assists secretion of bile
	leaf	IV.—V.	in salads, soups, sauces, as substitution for spinach	
	flower	V.	for syrup, wine	
Thymus serpyllum Breckland Thyme	tops	V.—VIII.	to season soups, vegetable dishes, meats, sauces, stuffings, pulses, baked dishes	improves digestion, appetite, in diseases of respiratory tract
Thymus vulgaris Garden Thyme	tops	V.—VI., VIII.—X.	to season bouillons, sauces, fish, game, poultry, pulses, pizzas, vegetables	in digestion disorders, disinfectant effects
Trapa natans Water Chestnut	fruit	X.—XI.	raw, boiled, roasted, ground to powder	high content of nutritious substances

plant	collected part	month of collection	use in kitchen	medicinal effects
Tussilago farfara Colt's-foot	flower	III.—IV.	for syrups, teas, honey	for diseases of respiratory tract, cough, high blood pressure, digestive disorders
	leaf	V.—VI.	in soups, stuffings, for casings filled with a stuffing	
Urtica dioica Common Nettle	leaf	IV.—V.	as substitution for spinach, for soups, sauces, in stuffings, salads, minced meats, spreads, savoury desserts	promotes digestion, diuretic effects, assists secretion of bile
Urtica urens Small Nettle	leaf	V.—VI.	as substitution for spinach, in salads, stuffings, egg dishes, forcemeats, for soups	promotes digestion, production of blood, diuretic effects
Vaccinium myrtillus Bilberry	fruit	VII.—VIII.	for syrups, wines, liqueurs, compotes, jams, fruit sauces, soups, filling for desserts	disinfectant, anti-diarrhoea effects
	leaf	V.—VIII.	for tea	
Vaccinium oxycoccos Cranberry	fruit	IX.—XI. III.	for preserves, juices, syrups, compotes, in honey, sauce with game	diuretic effects, assists secretion of bile, to cure common cold
	leaf	VI.—XI.	for tea	
Vaccinium vitis-idaea Cowberry	fruit	VI.—IX.	for compotes with game, sauces, jams	improves digestion, appetite, with kidney and urinary tract disorders, to check diarrhoea
	leaf	VI.—IX.	for tea	
Valerianella locusta Lamb's Lettuce	leaf	III.—IV., IX.—X.	in omelets, salads, soups, spreads	promotes digestion, calming effects
Viburnum opulus Guelder-rose	fruit	X.—XI.	for compotes, juices, syrups, preserves, sauces, filling for desserts	antispasmodic, calming effects, to cure common cold
Viola odorata Sweet Violet	leaf	III.—IV.	in herb soups, sauces, omelets	to lower blood pressure, to check diseases of respiratory tract
	flower	III.—IV.	for syrups, oil	

COLOUR PLATES

Yarrow
Achillea millefolium
Compositae/Asteraceae

Yarrow is a common plant native to Europe, growing in dry meadows, pastures, by the edges of fields and roads from lowlands to mountainous regions. It grows also in Asia and was introduced to North America, Australia and New Zealand. Yarrow has been used in medicine since ancient times, being mentioned in the writings of Hippocrates, Pliny the Elder and Dioscorides, and in the Middle Ages it took its place alongside other important drugs. The young leaves, picked early in spring before the stems are formed, can be chopped and added to omelets, sauces and soups. They are aromatic and have a bitterish and spicy flavour. The stem tops can also be collected by cutting with scissors before the buds develop, or later the flowers with short stalks may be used. The fresh or dried flowers are used to spice food, having a bitterish peppery, slightly salty flavour. Yarrow contains volatile oils, up to 0.25 per cent, with chamazulene, flavonoides, bitters, tannins, choline, mucilages, inulin and a considerable quantity of minerals and organic acids. It has antispasmodic, anti-inflammatory and antibacterial effects. It aids the flow of digestive juices and thus improves digestion. It should be added to food only in small amounts and then not too frequently. When the normal and harmless dosage is exceeded it can cause dizziness or skin rashes.

Description

Yarrow (1) is a perennial, bitter-scented herb. Its creeping, branched rhizome produces shoots with leaves and flowering stems. The erect, densely leaved stems, which reach up to 80 cms in height, are covered with alternate, dark green, spear-shaped leaves bearing two to three leaflets with variously shaped and articulated segments. The inflorescence (2) forms dense flat-topped sprays composed of small flower heads (4) with fused envelopes. The properties of Yarrow do not depend on the colour of its flowers; even pink-flowering Yarrow (3) can be used. It flowers from June to September. The ligulate ray florets (4) are female, white to deep pink, the bisexual disk florets are white and five-petalled. The fruits are elongated, silvery grey seed pods with narrow, lateral wings.

3

30

Spring Herb Soup

Ingredients
A bowl of spring herbs (leaves of
nettles, sweet violet, strawberry, ground
ivy, yarrow, plantain, caraway, ground
elder, chives), 1.5 litres meat stock,
1 egg, 1 tbsp butter, ground pepper, salt,
croûtons to garnish

Method
Wash, cut and boil herbs for a short
time in the stock. Add butter and beat in
the egg. Season with salt and pepper
and serve with croûtons.

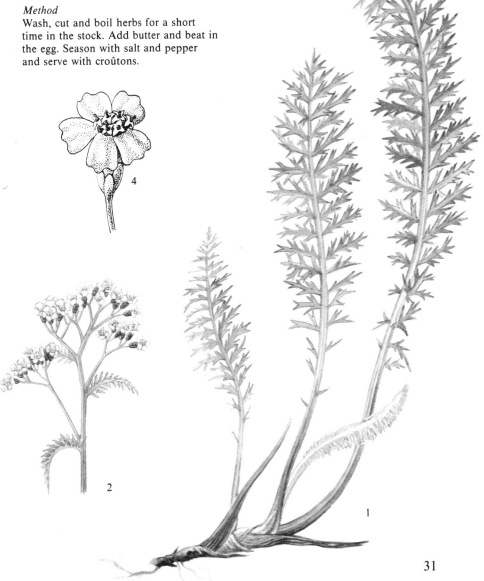

31

Sweet Flag
Acorus calamus

Araceae

Sweet flag is a native of southern China and India. It probably came to Europe via the Balkans with the Tartars and Turks, perhaps even with the crusaders. In the 16th century several plants were brought from India to the Viennese botanical gardens and today's distribution and domestication of sweet flag in central Europe is attributed to them. It grows in Eurasia, North America and the northern regions of the tropics, forming many natural races and varieties. In Europe the triploid type is most common. It is infertile here and multiplies only vegetatively by its rhizome, or subterranean root-stem. It is this rhizome which is collected for food use, being picked from the mud in autumn between September and November or in spring in the second and third year of growth. It is used fresh or dried. After being washed, it is sliced into 20—30 cm long pieces, the roots then being removed and the cut pieces dried or minced. Thick rhizomes are best halved and possibly peeled before being dried. Fresh rhizomes can be candied. Sweet flag is used to spice cordial liqueurs, fruit soups and sauces, sweet dishes and petit fours, wine sauces accompanying chicken, stewed apples and pears, brandies, teas, red cabbage and other vegetables, or added to ginger, mace or cinnamon. It has a sharp, aromatic scent and a bitter, spicy flavour, and is best used in small quantities, a slice of the rhizome being sufficient. Young, early spring shoots can be made into a salad to stimulate the appetite. The rhizome of the sweet flag contains an aromatic volatile oil, sugars, choline, mucilages, bitter principles, vitamin C and other substances. It aids metabolism and is effective in treating digestive disorders, abdominal pains, flatulence and poor appetite.

Description

Sweet flag is a perennial marsh herb, growing in large colonies at the margins of ponds, streams, in blind river arms, in large ditches and marshes from lowland areas to mountainous regions. Its stout, long rhizome with numerous smooth roots (1) creeps along the surface of the mud. The rhizome produces sabre-shaped leaves up to 1 metre long and a single flower stalk (2). The small yellow-green flowers are tightly packed into a cylindrical enclosed spike which seemingly grows from the side of the stem; the flower stalk is similar to the leaf in shape and grows upright in the direction of the stem. The fruit is a red berry containing several seeds which in Europe fail to ripen.

32

Pear Compote with Sweet Flag

Ingredients
1 kg pears, 5 cm long sweet flag
rhizome, 150 g sugar, 1 l water

Method
Peel and halve pears and remove cores.
Place in a pan, add sweet flag and
water, boil for a short time, add sugar
and cook until tender. Cool the compote
and remove sweet flag before serving.

2

1

33

Goutweed, Ground Elder
Aegopodium podagraria

Umbelliferae

This is commonly found in shady places, especially in gardens where it forms a continuous ground cover. Its leaves and rhizomes have an aromatic scent reminiscent of carrot. It has a characteristic appearance and there is no possibility that it might be confused with another plant. Goutweed is widespread in Europe, western and central Asia and also North America, where it was introduced. It grows in thickets, along fences, in damp forests, alongside streams and in gardens, particularly in shady places. It is a very aggressive weed. Edible parts are the young undeveloped shoots with leaves and petioles (the slender stalk which joins the leaf-blade to the stem). They can be collected throughout the period of growth. It is used in the preparation of soups and salads, preferably in a mixture with other herbs or vegetables. Goutweed contains mineral compounds, particularly calcium, magnesium and iron, and when young, the leaves contain a lot of carotene and vitamin C (about 70 mg in 100 g).

Description

Goutweed (1) is a perennial herb which multiplies through its very hardy, profusely branching rhizomes. Every piece of the rhizome, after being cut, has the potential to develop into a new plant, but its reproduction through the seeds is less common. It grows best in fertile soils with a sufficient amount of nitrogen and moisture. The rhizome produces the basal leaves (2), which grow on long, grooved leaf stalks and are divided into two to three leaflets. Their segments are broadly spear-shaped and pointed, with coarsely serrated edges. The stems (3 — cross section of the stem) are erect, branched, hollow, grooved, and may reach a height of 80 cms. The stem leaves are divided into three leaflets. The leaf stalk broadens into a sheath at the base. The umbrella-shaped flower sprays consist of between 10 and 20 smaller flowers (4) and appear at the ends of the branches on coarsely hairy stalks. The flowers (5) are white or pinkish and have heart-shaped petals. Goutweed flowers from May to July, sometimes even later. The fruits (6) are egg shaped, laterally depressed seed pods reminiscent of caraway.

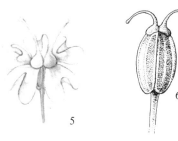

5

6

Braised Goutweed

Ingredients
800 g goutweed leaves, 3 tbsp oil,
3 onions, 3 cloves of garlic, a pinch of
ground mace, 3 potatoes, salt,
3 tbsp cream

Method
Wash leaves, scald in a strainer with
boiling water and leave to drain. Sauté
chopped onion and garlic in the oil, add
leaves and braise for a few minutes. Add
grated potatoes and cream, salt and
season with mace and cook stirring
continuously until the mixture thickens.
Serve with meat, boiled eggs or fish.

4

3

2

1

35

Lady's Mantle
Alchemilla xanthochlora

Rosaceae

Lady's mantle commonly grows in grassland, forming a rosette of cornet-shaped leaves often containing a characteristic droplet of dew in the middle. Alchemists used to collect it and attributed to it great medicinal powers. They named it 'heavenly dew' and put it to use when searching for the philosophers' stone. It is native to the temperate zone of Europe, western Asia, northern Africa and Canada, and has also been introduced in other places. Its young leaves, which have a characteristic smell and a rather astringent and bitterish taste, are edible. They should be collected before the plant starts to flower between May and September, and can be added to soups, spinach and vegetable side-dishes. They can be also made into a vitaminized drink in a dilution of 4 teaspoons per cup of liquid. Lady's mantle has about 200 mg vitamin C per 100 g leaves which is five times more than lemons. It also contains carotene and various mineral substances, in particular phosphorus, magnesium, calcium (as much as 8 per cent), tannins, bitter principles, mucilages, saponins, salicylic acid and various other substances. Lady's mantle is a popular medicinal herb with a long-standing reputation in folk medicine. It aids digestion and kidney function, and is recommended for gall-bladder and kidney stone complaints. Folk medicine recommends it particularly for gynaecological complaints to check heavy bleeding and problems of middle age. An extract made from lady's mantle is useful as a gargle to treat the inflammation of mucous membranes in the mouth, in baths or as a compress for slow healing wounds. Lady's mantle is also a component of teas used in slimming aids.

Description
Lady's mantle is a perennial, variable plant with a short, permanent rhizome growing close to the surface of the ground and with a rosette of basal leaves (1). It grows in damp meadows, at the margins of forests, pastureland, alongside waterways, in wet ground from low to high altitudes. It forms a dense ground cover in well-nourished soil and overwhelms other plants. It is mainly spread by animals when grazing.

36

2

The leaves (2, 3 — underside) are tough, rounded and lobed, being fluted when young. Their edges are serrate and the surface is glossy and densely hairy. The erect, leafy stems are 30 cm tall and branched at the top. The flowers, coloured an indistinct greenish yellow, open from May to September, forming sparse umbrella-shaped flower sprays with their top parts arranged in single flowers. The fruit is a seed pod enclosed in a persistent cup-shaped receptacle.

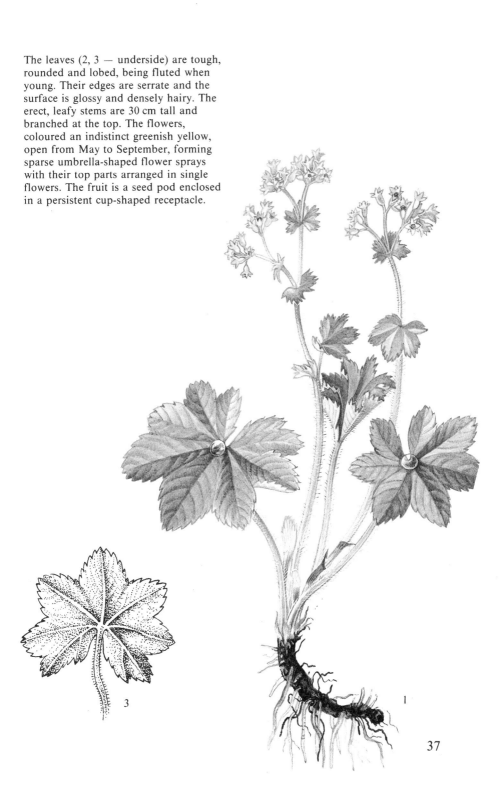

3

1

37

Garlic Mustard
Alliaria petiolata

Cruciferae

Garlic mustard is a weed growing in shady places. Its leaves have a characteristic garlic smell, particularly apparent when rubbed between the fingers, and possess a sharp burning taste. Its typical garlic aroma excludes any possibility of it being confused with any other species. Garlic mustard is especially widespread in Europe and western Asia. The young plant tops as well as the leaves and seeds are edible. Garlic Mustard is collected from spring until autumn. It can be added to dishes as a fresh, finely chopped ingredient. It is suitable whenever garlic is used, namely in soups, sauces, potato cakes, soft cheese spreads, stuffings, in dishes prepared with minced meat, with lamb and in vegetable salads. The fresh leaves can be exchanged for a powder obtained from its crushed seeds. All parts of the plant are imbued with an essential oil containing sulphur and ammonia along with tannins, phytoncides, enzymes and other substances, as well as being a source of calcium, phosphorus and iron. Its young tops have a high vitamin C content (about 170 mg in 100 g of fresh matter). It is an old medicinal herb having a marked antispasmodic and disinfectant effect on the digestive tract. It is used in treating chronic intestinal disorders and intestinal parasites. The juice from fresh leaves has a beneficial effect in cases of inflammatory and fungus diseases of the skin. It is recommended as a component of herbal cures to treat spring fatigue.

2

Description
Garlic Mustard (1) is a biennial to perennial herb. It grows in shady places in deciduous and mixed forests, in thickets, neglected gardens and parks, alongside roads and on wasteland. It thrives from lowlands to lower mountain elevations. Most herbivorous animals avoid it because of its powerful odour. In its first year it forms tufts of long-stalked leaves. In the second year an erect, simple or sparsely branched stem, as much as 1 metre in height, develops early in spring. The stem leaves (2) are narrow, smooth with short stalks,

triangular, and irregularly serrate along the edges. Small sprays of white flowers terminate the main stem and lateral branches. These lengthen considerably as the plant develops. The flowers open from April until the end of June. The fruit is an elongated, narrow pod with small round seeds. The seeds easily fall out of the ripe pods and are dispersed by rainwater.

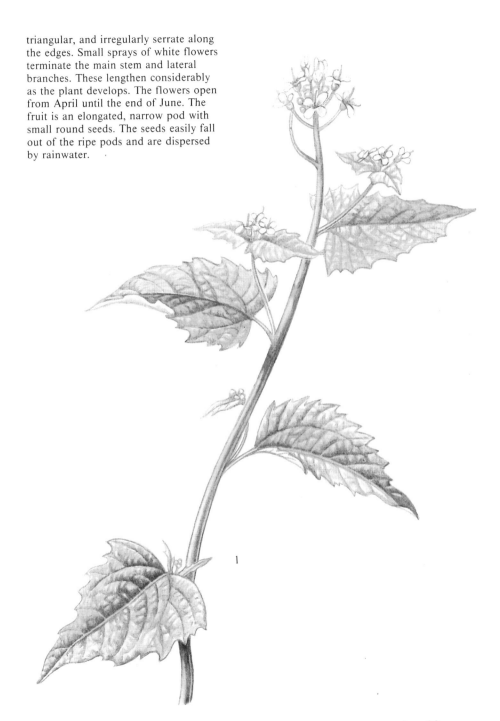

1

Chives
Allium schoenoprasum

Liliaceae

Wild and garden chives have been used in the kitchen since ancient times. In central Europe it has been cultivated since the 16th century. It grows wild in Europe, in Siberia, Kamchatka and also in North America. Elsewhere it has escaped from cultivation and reverted to its wild form. In Europe two wild species of chives are to be found, *A. schoenoprasum* ssp. *schoenoprasum* and *A. schoenoprasum* ssp. *sibiricum*. They have thinner tubular leaves and a sharper flavour than cultivated chives. Chives are an important source of vitamin C, containing 100 mg per 100 g of leaves. They also contain carotene, vitamins B_1 and B_2, a volatile oil with sulphur, phytoncides, calcium, potassium, phosphorus and iron. Chives stimulate the secretion of digestive juices, improve the appetite and slightly lower the blood pressure. In spring it is a particularly important source of necessary vitamins. It is used in the same way as cultivated chives. The young leaves are picked in April and May when they develop in dense tufts from small bulbs. It is best used fresh and is best preserved by freezing. Dried chives lose their scent and biological value. It is added to dishes finely chopped, always after boiling or sprinkled on food before serving. It can be added to soups, cream sauces, egg dishes, vegetable salads or as an accompaniment to potatoes, rice and pasta, in mayonnaise, spreads (e.g. with parsley, cress), in herb butter, cheese and cottage cheese spreads etc.

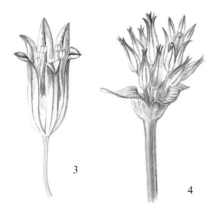

Description
Chives (1) is a perennial, frost-resistant herb. The roots of its elongated bulbs grow to a depth of 30 cm. Large tufts of chives have as many as 100 shoots with between two and four tubular leaves (2). The leaves appear in early spring and about 2 months later purple flowers (3) develop. They are arranged in umbrella-shaped sprays (4), each containing 100 or more tiny flowers. The flower stalk is hollow, erect, and reaches a height of up to 35 cm. Cutting the leaves prevents the formation of flowers.

40

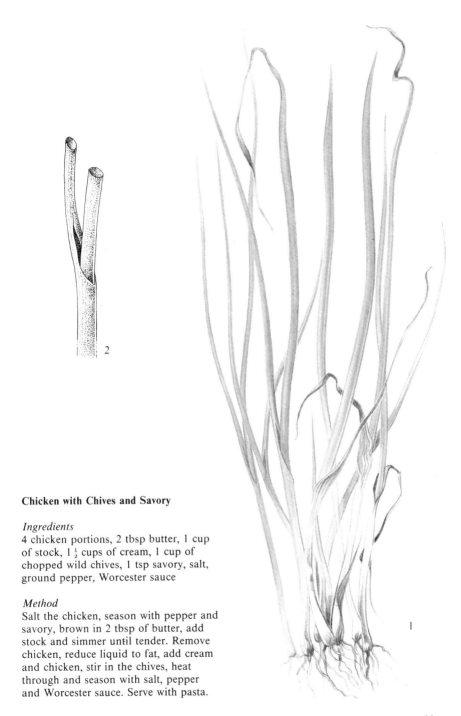

Chicken with Chives and Savory

Ingredients
4 chicken portions, 2 tbsp butter, 1 cup
of stock, 1 $\frac{1}{2}$ cups of cream, 1 cup of
chopped wild chives, 1 tsp savory, salt,
ground pepper, Worcester sauce

Method
Salt the chicken, season with pepper and
savory, brown in 2 tbsp of butter, add
stock and simmer until tender. Remove
chicken, reduce liquid to fat, add cream
and chicken, stir in the chives, heat
through and season with salt, pepper
and Worcester sauce. Serve with pasta.

41

Wild Garlic, Ramsons
Allium ursinum
Liliaceae

Wild garlic has a stronger aroma than its cultivated forms. It also has similar but weaker medicinal properties. Its smell is particularly strong during flowering and therefore it can be easily identified at a distance. The smell is transferred to the milk and meat of any animals who may eat it. However, they usually avoid it. The aerial parts are collected before flowering, in April and May, and its bulbs in September and October, which means practically the whole plant can be used. The amount used varies according to purpose. It is used to spice salads, vegetable stews, pulses, sauces, stuffings, forcemeat, fish, spreads made from poultry, mayonnaise, herb butters and soups. Wild garlic contains a volatile oil with sulphur compounds and ammonia, phytoncides, bitters and vitamin C, and its leaves also contain carotene. It is used frequently in folk medicine. It regulates the function of the stomach, stimulates the digestive tract, destroys intestinal parasites, lessens cramp in muscles and speeds up the healing of external wounds. Folk medicine recommends it not only for the above-mentioned diseases but also for treating high blood pressure, influenza and arteriosclerosis. It is used in spring medicinal cures.

2

Description
Wild garlic (1) is a perennial herb with a small conical bulb (2) and a triangular stem (3 — cross-section) between 10 and 30 cms in height. It is believed by some to be a favourite of bears and hence the Latin specific name. Common throughout Europe, northern Asia and Siberia, it grows in damp or wet places and in slightly acid shady locations. It is prolific in permanently wet meadows and groves, flowering in April and May. The leaves grow directly from the bulb. Unlike cultivated garlic its leaves are oval, with long petioles, resembling those of lily of the valley. Its flower stalk terminates in a narrow umbrella-shaped spray of six-petalled flowers, enclosed by a short membranous sheath when young. The petals are white and longer than the stamens.

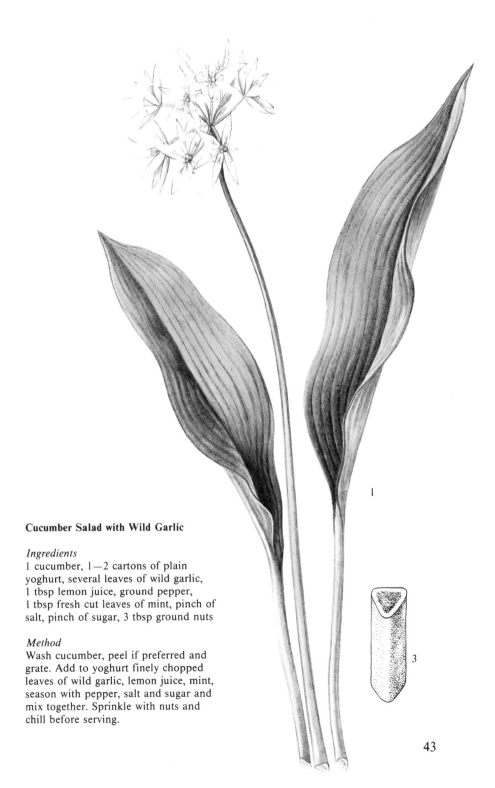

Cucumber Salad with Wild Garlic

Ingredients
1 cucumber, 1—2 cartons of plain
yoghurt, several leaves of wild garlic,
1 tbsp lemon juice, ground pepper,
1 tbsp fresh cut leaves of mint, pinch of
salt, pinch of sugar, 3 tbsp ground nuts

Method
Wash cucumber, peel if preferred and
grate. Add to yoghurt finely chopped
leaves of wild garlic, lemon juice, mint,
season with pepper, salt and sugar and
mix together. Sprinkle with nuts and
chill before serving.

Long-rooted Garlic
Allium victoriale

Liliaceae

Several species of wild garlic grow in Europe. Most abundant are wild garlic (p. 42) and sand leek (*A. scorodoprasum*) with many small bulbs in its collective flower. It grows in forests. Crow garlic or wild onions (*A. vineale*) are widespread in vineyards and gardens. It is considerably resilient to the environment and likes steppe conditions. Another species, *A. flavum,* can be found on dry grassy slopes in seaside regions. All wild garlics are edible. Long-rooted garlic is not very abundant in Europe. It is more common in Siberia, the Far East and in the Caucasus in subalpine meadows and in fir and pine forests. Its use is similar to that of wild garlic. The broad juicy leaves are eaten before the plant starts to flower between April and June, its bulbs developing in the autumn. It can be added to soups, sauces, salads, mayonnaise, spreads, served on grilled meats, with fish, poultry, lamb and pork. In Siberia it is used as a pie filling and its leaves are fermented in milk for winter as a vitamin supplement. The whole plant contains a volatile oil with sulphur, vitamin C, proteins, saccharides, phytoncides and other substances. The ancient Romans considered it to be a remedy for cleansing the stomach and the blood. Soldiers of the Roman legions ate it, believing that it healed wounds and strengthened courage. In folk medicine it is highly valued a remedy for scurvy and a diuretic medicine which stimulates the digestion and improves the appetite. In spring it is a source of necessary vitamins.

2

Description
Long-rooted garlic (1) is a perennial herb which reaches a height of 75 cms. In the ground it forms an egg-shaped bulb covered with brown intersecting scales. The leaves are flat, oval, light green, and between 3 and 6 cms wide. The flower stem (2 — cross-section) is erect and round and bears a globe-shaped terminal umbrella of white to green-yellow flowers between May and August.

Chicken with Herbs

Ingredients
1 chicken, 10 shallots, 5 leaves of
long-rooted garlic, a sprig of rosemary,
2 bay leaves, a pinch of fennel, 4 leaves
of sage, 3 sprigs of thyme, 1 cup of olive
oil, salt, ground pepper, 1 tbsp brandy

Method
Season the chicken with salt and pepper,
fry in oil, add herbs, shallots and
brandy, cover with a lid and braise for
1 hour. Add water as necessary. Serve
with white bread and vegetable salad.

1

45

Service-berry
Amelanchier ovalis

Rosaceae

The service-berry grows in central and southern Europe, in England, the Caucasus region, in western Asia and India and in North Africa. It is conspicuous in the flowering season and in autumn with its beautiful red leaves enhancing the limestone rocks on which it commonly grows. It can also be found in parks and gardens, from which it often escapes. Its sweet, juicy fruits are edible and contain about 10 per cent sugars, about 1 per cent acids, in particular malic acid, carotene, vitamin C, group B vitamins and minerals. In terms of trace elements it contains copper which is beneficial to the human body. The fruit also contains coumarin. The fruits are eaten fresh, or they can be made into jams, jellies, marmalades, juices and wines. They can also be dried and used as substitutes for raisins. They are also used in folk medicine, being recommended in the treatment of hypovitaminosis and as an infusion to treat sore throats and the common cold. The leaves and bark are used in preparing a tea to treat illnesses of the digestive tract. Some 25 species of the genus *Amelanchier* are known. Besides *A. ovalis* and *A. spicata,* edible fruits are also produced by *A. lamarckii* and some others.

Description
The service-berry is a tall shrub or a small tree. It has oval leaves, rounded at the tip, serrated along the edges, dark green on the top and light green on the underside. White five-petalled flowers are arranged in terminal clusters of between 3 and 6 flowers (1). They are white, sometimes reddish at the tip with a bell-shaped calyx. The fruits (2) ripen in autumn before the arrival of the first frosts. They are bluish black and round with a frosted appearance similar to that of a plum, 1 cm in diameter, with dry remnants of the calyx on the top. They are juicy, sweet and contain between four and ten seeds.

1

2

47

Angelica
Angelica archangelica

Umbelliferae

The occurrence of angelica has been considerably reduced in the wild by careless collection. However, this stout herb which sometimes reaches a height of two metres can be still found in the damp terrain of submountainous regions. As early as the 17th century it was one of the medicinal and spicy ingredients of Benedictine and Chartreuse liqueurs. It is used as a spice, a vegetable and a medicine. Its roots, rhizomes, young leaves, stems and seed pods are all edible. All parts of the plant have a strong aroma and sharp spicy, slightly bitter taste. The young leaves and stems should be collected in May and June and the fruit in September. Roots and rhizomes can be dug up in the autumn or even better in March and April when they contain as much as 1.5 per cent essential oil. The young shoots are used to flavour salads, soups, sauces, vegetables, whilst the young flowering stalks and petioles are cut into small pieces, candied and used to decorate petit fours. The seeds are used as a spice. Angelica provides a raw material for the production of an essential oil, used in perfumery and the food industry and to aromatize snuff. In addition to essential oil it contains furocoumarin, flavonoides, organic acids (malic, valeric, methyl acetic), bitter principles, resin, tannins, sugars, wax and other substances. The fruits have the highest content of essential oil and the stems the lowest, but they contain vitamin C and carotene. In popular medicine angelica is regarded as a universal cure-all. It has antibacterial and diuretic effects as well as aiding digestion and the activity of the digestive tract. However, it is not recommended as a regular ingredient as it contains coumarin elements which in sensitive people can cause an oversensitive response to the sun and even an allergic skin reaction.

Description
Angelica (1) is a robust herb with a beet-like rhizome (2) and numerous brown roots. It dies off after flowering. In the first year of its growth it forms a large rosette of long-stalked basal leaves; this is followed in the second year by a stem with large, triangular, stemless leaves enclosed at the base by a swollen sheath. The stem is thick, hollow, grooved, red-brown in colour, branching only in the upper part. Its

20—40 flowers are arranged in an umbrella-shaped spray (3) which appears in July and August. The flowers are bisexual, radial, greenish to yellowish. The fruit is a double pod (4) which splits into two yellowish winged seed pods. Angelica grows in damp, light thickets, alongside woodland streams and springs from submountain to mountain regions. It is widespread in the temperate zone of Europe and Asia, but in the south only in the mountains. It is cultivated in some countries but often reverts to its wild form.

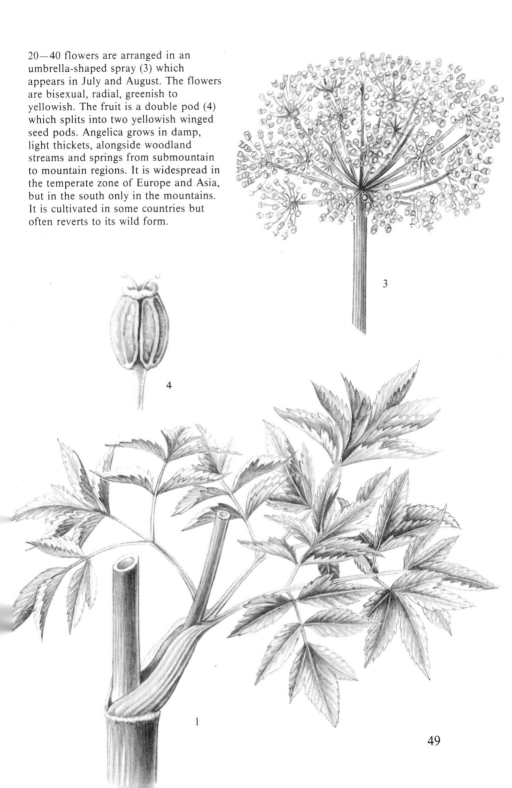

3

4

1

49

Great Burdock
Arctium lappa

On a country walk the hooked burrs or fruits of great burdock often become attached to our clothes. Similarly they also stick to animal fur. This is the way in which great burdock spreads. It has been known to popular medicine from ancient times and is surrounded by superstition and magic. Great burdock has been used as a hair restorer since the Middle Ages and is common in Europe and Asia and has also been introduced in America. In the Far East it is cultivated as a root vegetable. It is particularly popular in Japan and China. Its roots and leaves are edible, the young leaves being added to soups and salads. The roots are dug up in autumn or spring and are grated when fresh and used both raw and cooked. They have a juicy, bittersweet flavour. Roasted and minced roots can be used as a coffee substitute. The roots contain polysaccharide inulin (40—50 per cent) and therefore great burdock is used to treat diabetes in its early stages. It also contains proteins, glycoside arctiin, volatile oil, mucilage, tannins, bitter principles, phytoncides, resins, aliphatic oil, calcium, potassium and phosphorus. Its leaves contain vitamin C (as much as 350 mg per 100 g). The root of great burdock has perspiratory, diuretic and antibacterial effects. In folk medicine it is used for digestive disorders, in catarrh of the stomach and illnesses associated with ulcers, in kidney and urinary diseases; it is used externally in infusions for bathing eczemas and wounds which are slow to heal. Oil macerations are used in cosmetics to slow down hair loss.

Description
Great burdock (1) is a biennial plant, growing to a height of 180 cm with a massive, branched root (2). It is collected only in the first year of its growth in autumn or in the second year in spring since it later becomes too woody to use. It grows on wasteland, tips, pastureland, alongside roads, fences, mainly in the vicinity of human habitation in a soil enriched with nitrogen. It is a native of the temperate zone and northern subtropics. In the first year it forms a rosette of large basal leaves. An erect, stout, profusely branched, furrowed and woolly, often reddish, swollen stem develops in the second year. Its leaves are alternate, oval to heart-shaped and grey-cottony beneath. The red spherical heads form long clusters and have bracts equipped with bent hooks (3). They flower in July and August and the flowers have a purple corolla (4). The fruit is a black seed pod with several rows of soft hair. Two other related species, namely *A. tomentosum* and *A. minor,* can be used to a similar effect.

1

2

3

4

51

Horse-radish
Armoracia rusticana

Cruciferae

Horse-radish is an age old multi-purpose and medicinal plant. For ages past it has been used especially by Slavs and Germans. It has been cultivated in central Europe since the 12th century and the first recipes for horse-radish sauce date back to that time. Horse-radish still grows wild in the south-eastern European part of the USSR and in western Asia. At present it is cultivated throughout Europe but often reverts to its wild form. Wild horse-radish forms vast covers in damp thickets, along waterways and in the vicinity of human habitation. It can prove a most valuable component of our diet in winter and in spring. It contains a sharp, bitter volatile oil (up to 2 per cent) with glycoside sinigrin, sugars, up to 100 mg of vitamin C in 100 g, carotene, vitamins of group B, phytoncides with antibacterial effects, minerals and other elements. When cooked it loses its qualities and should therefore be consumed freshly grated. It has a sharp, specific smell, acrid taste and causes the eyes to water. The grated root is served with boiled meat, smoked meat products, fish, hard-boiled eggs and is used to flavour sauces and spreads. A mixture of grated horse-radish and apples is a favourite accompaniment of boiled meat, smoked meat products, game etc. Young horse-radish leaves can be used in pickling vegetables (gherkins, beetroot) and finely chopped in soups. Horse-radish goes well with fattier dishes as it improves digestion. However, it should not be consumed in large quantities; 1—2 tbsp of finely grated horse-radish per person is sufficient.

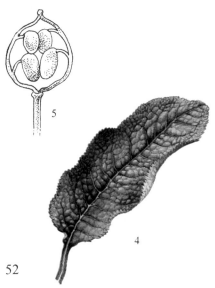

5

4

Description
Horse-radish is a perennial, frost-resistant plant. Its yellowish white root (1, 2 — lengthwise section) produces erect, leafy stems growing up to 1 $\frac{1}{2}$ metres in height and branched at the top. The basal leaves (4) are large with long stalks, the stem leaves being smaller and having no stalk at all. The stem terminates in a loose, irregular spray of white, scented flowers (3), which are present from May to July. The fruits are spherical (5 — cross section), containing flat seeds. Horse-radish usually multiplies vegetatively by its roots which are harvested in the autumn. It requires

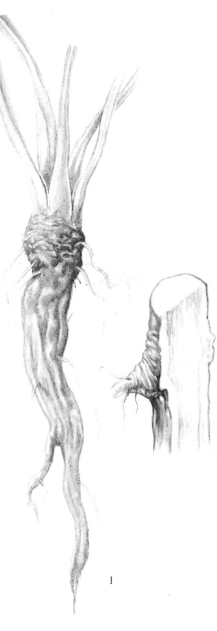

and it is therefore better to use the cultivated varieties which are less sharp and have a sweetish taste. Horse-radish has long been attributed with medicinal properties and it is used extensively in popular medicine.

Horse-radish with Apples

Ingredients
$\frac{1}{2}$ kg apples, 25—50 g horse-radish, 1 tbsp sugar, juice of $\frac{1}{2}$ lemon

Method
Peel apples, clean horse-radish, grate finely and mix with sugar and lemon juice. Mixture is pressed into a glass container and closed.

a light, sandy soil, and after harvesting, the root is kept in soil in a frame or in sand in the cellar. Horse-radish which has reverted to its wild form has a higher content of pungent volatile oil

1

2

3

Garden Orache
Atriplex hortensis
Chenopodiaceae

Orache probably originated from shining orache (*A. nitens*). It is a native of southern Europe and the regions stretching from the Caucasus across central Asia to Siberia, and does not grow in northern Europe. It can be found in three different colour variations, namely with either yellowish green, bright green or deep red leaves. These are very decorative and are therefore cultivated as decorative annuals. Orache can be often found in the wild having escaped from gardens. Other oraches are also edible, for example the common orache (*A. patula*) and shining orache (*A. nitens*). It was recognized as a vegetable by the ancient Mediterranean civilisations and was also used frequently in the medieval kitchen having since been replaced by spinach. One of the advantages of orache is that it does not require any specialized location. Its leaves can be collected over a longer period than those of spinach, and they have a more delicate flavour since they contain only a small quantity of oxalic acid. The young plants are usually collected in April and May. They are edible even later but are more fibrous when in flower. Apart from a small quantity of oxalic acid orache contains about 18 per cent dry matter, 5 per cent proteins and over 7 per cent saccharides. It is very rich in minerals, particularly calcium and magnesium, containing also phosphorus, iron and a large quantity of vitamin C — about 150 mg per 100 g. Carotene is also present along with other vegetable pigments, such as anthocyan in the red form. During cooking the colour is released into the water and the leaves turn green. Orache is prepared in the same way as spinach. It can be also added to soups, stuffings, forcemeat, egg dishes etc. Orache is one of nature's high fibre foods and also plays a part in the formation of the blood.

Description
Orache (1) is an annual plant. Its stems reach a height of about 1 metre and are slightly branched. The leaves (2) are shaped like a spearhead, either entirely or slightly tooth-edged, dull, with a fine surface and the same colour on both sides. The young leaves are covered with tiny white hairs so that they appear as if dusted with flour. The yellowish or red flowers are arranged in rich clusters and

54

open from July to September. The fruits
are flat seed pods and as the plant
produces a great number of them, it can
survive in one location in large
quantities if the conditions are
favourable for self-seeding. The seeds
lose their ability to germinate after the

second year. Orache can be harvested
about two months after sowing as it
grows very quickly. It is a modest but
highly productive plant. When gathering
it, dense growths should be avoided; the
best quality leaves are produced by
plants under half a metre in height.

1

Daisy
Bellis perennis

This tiny popular perennial plant flowers almost all year round. It is widespread throughout most of Europe, reaching as far as Asia Minor and has been introduced and become naturalized in North America and New Zealand. In the Middle Ages it was one of the universally used medicines and its young leaves were already used as a lettuce or spinach substitute. The daisy contains a volatile oil, saponins, tannins, flavonoides, mucilages, about 2 per cent protein, saccharides, carotene, about 30 mg vitamin C per 100 g—about the same as lemons—as well as other substances. It also possesses anti-inflammatory and expectorant qualities and a liquid prepared from flowers can be used in the treatment of coughs, congestion in the respiratory tract and rheumatism. This liquid can also be applied externally in the treatment of slowly healing wounds, bruises and to prevent bleeding. The daisy is no longer widely used as a herb but is still recognized as being beneficial to human health. The leaf rosettes with flower buds attached are a valuable source of vitamin C in early spring. It can be prepared as a salad with onion or sorrel and can be also added to the potato salad, herb butter, soups, sauces, stuffings, spreads, omelets etc. The flower buds can be pickled in vinegar like capers. The flowers can be used to decorate dishes, lemonade and milk drinks and a syrup to treat the common cold can be prepared from them.

Daisy Syrup

Ingredients
250 g daisy flowers, ½ lemon, 40 g castor sugar, 3—4 cups of water

Method
Scald flowers with boiling water, add slices of lemon and leave to steep. The following day strain the liquid through a piece of muslin, add sugar and boil until thick. Add syrup to tea to treat common colds.

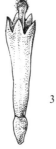

3

2

Description

Daisy (1) is a perennial herb with a cylindrical rootstock and a rosette of basal leaves. The stalked leaves vary from being oval shaped with a narrower end at the base to spathulate, edged in rounded teeth. An erect stem which reaches a height of 20 cms and terminates a single flower head grows from the leaf rosette. The plants form small clusters and are commonly found in pastureland, meadows, on grassy banks, and alongside roads from lowland to mountain elevations. It flowers in early spring, again in autumn and sometimes even under snow in winter. The flower heads consist of white male ray florets (2), often with the tips tinged reddish, and yellow bisexual disk florets (3). The ray florets bend inward at night or in rainy weather, so that they close the whole head. The fruits are smooth seed pods. Cultivated varieties are often grown in gardens and seeds are added to grass mixtures to make decorative lawns.

1

Barberry
Berberis vulgaris

Berberidaceae

The barberry belongs to a large genus including some 170 species. It is widespread in central Europe, Greece, Spain, in the Caucasus, in central and south-western Asia. In the past its fruit was collected by people living in Babylon and India, and the Arabs called it *berberis*. In the Middle Ages it was recommended for the treatment of jaundice and malaria and is still of importance in this respect. The fruits are collected in September and October, just before they are fully ripe, red in colour and firm, otherwise they get spoiled. Unripe fruits should not be collected. The fruits contain about 5 per cent sugars, 6.5 per cent organic acids (mainly malic, citric and tartaric), pectins, 150 mg vitamin C per 100 g (3 times more than lemons), vitamin E, provitamin A and other substances. The juice is rich in vitamins and has mild laxative effects. It aids digestion, stimulates the appetite and secretion of bile and has diuretic effects. The plant, apart from the ripe fruits, contains the alkaloid berberin, which is highly toxic and should only be used under medical supervision. The fruits have a slightly acid flavour, and can be used fresh and dried in the same way as rosehips. Tea made from dried barberries is consumed to combat fatigue and common cold. The fresh fruit can be frozen (dusted with sugar) or can be made into syrup, wine, tea, liqueurs, compotes and jam. Its juice, like lemon juice, can be used to flavour salads. The fresh fruit can be added to preserves made from insipid-tasting fruit such as mulberries, apples and pears. It can also be preserved in honey and used to treat fever. Dried powdered fruits may be used to flavour sauces, soups, game and grilled meat. The powder should be kept in tightly closed jars in a dry and dark place.

Description
Barberry (1) is a spiny shrub which may reach a height of 3 metres. It can be found growing wild in thickets, on dry slopes and banks, and is often used in parks as an ornamental shrub. As it is a host of several dangerous parasitic fungi belonging to the rust group, it often has to be removed from the vicinity of fields. For this reason it has been almost eradicated from the wild in central Europe. It tolerates dry conditions well and limestone substrata at lower altitudes. At higher altitudes it is even bound to limestone. The leaves (2) are alternate, serrated on the edge and arranged in clusters. They develop in the angle between spines and branches. The flowers, which appear from May to June, are yellow and arranged in hanging clusters. The fruits (3), tiny, oval berries with 2—3 seeds containing up to 15 per cent oil, ripen between September and October.

58

2

3

1

Silver Birch
Betula pendula
Betulaceae

Silver birch grows in central and northern Europe and in western Siberia, predominantly in the temperate zone. In the south it also grows in the Pyrenees, Sicily, the Caucasus and northern Iran. In Finland and the Soviet Union it forms continuous woodland colonies. Its aromatic and delicious juice is acquired by drilling the trees to a depth of 2—3 cm in spring when the pressure of the rising sap is strong. The quantity of juice extracted from a mature tree is quite large, $1-1\frac{1}{2}$ litres per day. The sap in the main consists of water and sugars (fructosis), but also minerals, volatile oil, tannins, flavonoides and vitamin C. In its unadulterated state it may be consumed as a refreshing drink or it can be made into a syrup or fermented with sugar as 'birch Champagne'. Boiled with wine (2 dcl white wine and 2 tbsp juice), it is used to treat stomach cramp and intestinal colic. Birch juice can only be extracted in places with extensive birch growth since the drilling of the stems damages the tree, and is therefore not permitted in most central European countries. However, juice can be extracted from trees designated for felling. Birch juice is used in cosmetics and as a hair tonic. In folk medicine its leaves or leaf buds are used; the leaf buds have up to 5 per cent volatile oil, the leaves less than 1 per cent. The volatile oil has a use in the production of perfumes. The leaves also contain saponins, bitter principles, yellow pigment, sugars, malic and citric acid, vitamin C and B, carotene and others. The infusion prepared from the leaves has a powerful diuretic efffect. It is used to treat kidney diseases, rheumatism and externally for invigorating baths and regenerating the complexion.

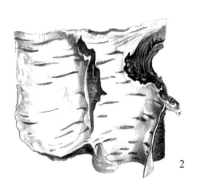

2

Description
The birch (1) is a tall, slender tree with at first erect and later pendent branches. It carries unisexual male and female organs on the same plant and grows in light woods, clearings, on slopes and rocks from the lowlands to high altitudes, occasionally even up to the alpine belt. It prefers acid infertile soils with a sufficient amount of light, otherwise it has no specific demands, being unusually hardy. It is planted in parks and to cover infertile land, spoil heaps, wasteland and tips thrown up after mining. The bark is white and smooth above (2) and dark and fissured towards the base. The white bark peels

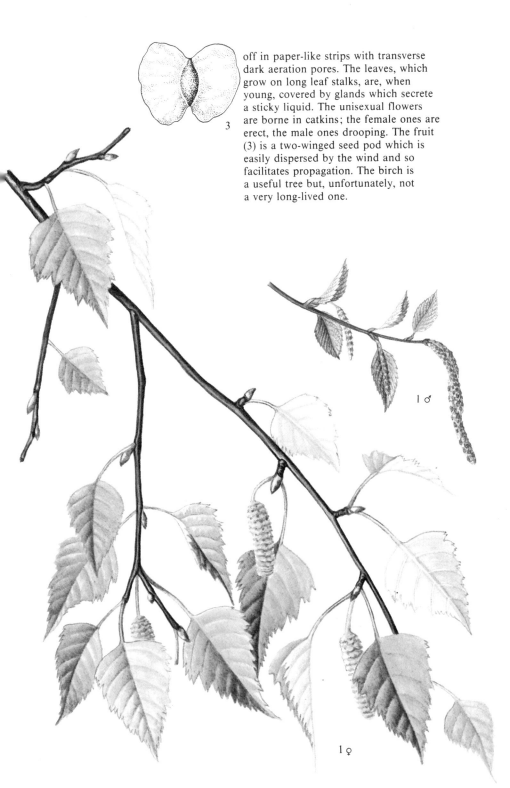

off in paper-like strips with transverse
dark aeration pores. The leaves, which
grow on long leaf stalks, are, when
young, covered by glands which secrete
a sticky liquid. The unisexual flowers
are borne in catkins; the female ones are
erect, the male ones drooping. The fruit
(3) is a two-winged seed pod which is
easily dispersed by the wind and so
facilitates propagation. The birch is
a useful tree but, unfortunately, not
a very long-lived one.

3

1 ♂

1 ♀

Borage
Borago officinalis
Boraginaceae

The origins of borage are not known. Ancient Mediterraneans probably had no idea of its possible uses or medicinal properties. The first to cultivate it, in the Middle Ages, may have been the Arabs who inhabited southern Spain. Nowadays, it also grows in the warmer regions of western, central and eastern Europe and in western Asia and it has also been introduced to other continents. It is commonly cultivated in gardens from where it often escapes into the wild. The young leaves and flowers are edible: the leaves can be picked from the basal leaf rosettes when their hairs are still soft. Older leaves and tops can be dried for medicinal purposes. They contain mostly mucilages (up to 30 per cent), resin, malic and citric acid, tannins, saponins, the pigment anthocyanin and also minerals, e. g. potassium, calcium and manganese. Fresh leaves have a relatively high content of vitamin C (up to 20 mg per 100 g), and they smell and taste like fresh cucumbers. The finely chopped leaves may be used as a tasty ingredient added to salads containing tomato, potato and cucumber, in vegetable and meat dishes, cold sauces and soups, soft cheese spreads, mayonnaise, herb butters, forcemeats, with fish and to flavour cold drinks, or can simply be sprinkled on bread and butter. The young leaves can be prepared sautéed with onion and butter just like spinach or can be used as a filling for pies and ravioli. An essence extracted from the leaves is used to colour dull green tinned vegetables. The flowers may be used to decorate fruit soups, salads and desserts, and can also be candied and used to aromatize herb vinegar. The dried leaves are unsuitable as spice as they lose their aroma. Borage has diuretic, mild laxative, disinfectant and anti-inflammatory properties. It is used for the treatment of nervous exhaustion and depression; freshly pressed juice from the leaves is used in spring cures.

Description

Borage (1) is a robust annual, reaching a height of between 50 and 70 cm. It has a simple or branching stem, often with a reddish hue at the top, growing in damp, sandy to clay soils in full sun or semishade. It is not a demanding species but plants growing in fertile soil are more robust. It easily seeds itself out and escapes into the wild. It is also cultivated in gardens as a decorative plant. The flowers secrete a considerable

2

amount of nectar and borage is thus
considered an important plant in the
production of honey. Its stems and
leaves are covered with coarse bristly
hairs. The azure blue, white or reddish
flowers on long stalks are arranged in
sparse monochasial sprays opening from
May to September. The fruits (2) are
four ovoid brown nutlets which
contain oil.

1

Pot Marigold
Calendula officinalis

Compositae

Pot marigold is commonly cultivated in gardens from where it often escapes to the wild, and is native to the western Mediterranean. It was mentioned for the first time as a medicinal herb in the 12th century by the famous abbess and herbalist Hildegarde of Bingen. Its scientific generic name comes from the Latin word *calendae,* according to the Romans the first day of the month (hence the word calendar). The deep orange ray florets have long been used as a substitute for saffron and as a harmless natural food colouring, for example in butter and cheeses. They can also be used in the same way as saffron to add colour to soups, sauces, doughs and rice, or added to tea to improve its appearance. They have a slightly bitter, salty flavour and contain mainly volatile oil, saponins, a bitter principle called calendin, carotenoids, flavonoids, mucilages, phytoncides, vitamin C, fats, resins, salicylic acid and other substances. Its young leaves are also edible and can be added to soups and salads. The pot marigold has anti-inflammatory, diuretic, perspiratory and anticonvulsive effects. It is used to treat digestive disorders, inflammations of the gall-bladder and urinary bladder; it is used externally in baths to treat skin diseases and heal wounds. In medicinal cosmetics it is used in preparations which make the skin softer and supple and is added to baths. The freshly pressed juice also has medicinal properties.

Description

Pot marigold (1) is an annual and occasionally a biennial plant. It grows in the wild in regions stretching from the Mediterranean to Iran and is cultivated as a decorative, honey producing, medicinal plant. Its stems are erect, up to 50 cms tall, branching at the apex and terminating in a cluster of flowers. The leaves are elongated, alternate, appearing sticky and coarse to the touch. It flowers from May until late autumn. The flower heads are surrounded by a two-tier whorl of bracts; the ray florets are strap-shaped (2) and the disc florets are tubular (3).

The ray florets are light yellow to deep orange and in the disk range from yellow to brown. The fruit is smooth skinned, small and dry. The concern of the collector are the strap-shaped ray florets, which are picked from fresh plants at the point of full bloom. They should be dried quickly in the shade, and protected from dampness and light in which they become pale. Plants with simple yellow-orange coloured flower heads are mostly found in the wild, but the double-flowered garden varieties are also suitable for use in the kitchen.

1

2

3

65

Rampion
Campanula rapunculus
Campanulaceae

The leaves and roots of rampion have been in use since the Middle Ages. It is not very common in central Europe, more so in the wine-growing regions of Europe, Asia and Africa. Garden forms are also grown mainly in southern France. The carrot-like, edible roots are whitish inside. They are formed with a basal leaf rosette in the first year, containing inulin instead of starch, a large amount of minerals (calcium, iron, phosphorus), vitamins, mucilage, choline, gum and cellulose, and are particularly suitable for diabetics. They can be used in preparation of soups and side dishes or can be added to vegetable mixtures. The raw roots are coarsely grated and made into a delicious salad. Apart from the roots, its young leaves can be also eaten, if collected before the stem develops. A salad can be prepared from them, rich in vitamin C.

Description

Rampion (1) is a biennial plant. In the first year it forms a rosette of basal, long-stalked leaves with broad blades and serrated edges. In the ground it has a thick, carrot-like, white root with a white flesh, measuring up to 8 cm long and 2 cm wide. Sometimes it forms underground secondary small tubers from which new plants can be grown. In the second year an erect, unbranched, grooved, 30—80 cms tall stem grows out of the root. From May it produces blue bell-shaped flowers (3), arranged in a narrow loose inflorescence. One third of the corolla is divided into bell-shaped lobes. The fruit is a capsule with small seeds. Rampion is chiefly propagated vegetatively. For germination the seeds require dispersed light and germinate on the surface of the soil. Despite the fact that Rampion is predominantly widespread in warm, wine-growing regions, its root is quite frost-resistant.

Salad from Rampion Roots

Ingredients

500 g fresh root, 2 tbsp oil, 2 tbsp vinegar, 1 tbsp chopped chives, ground pepper, salt

Method
Clean and coarsely grate the roots. Add oil, vinegar and chives, stir, season with salt and pepper and allow to cool.

1

2

Stemless Thistle
Carlina acaulis
Compositae

In ancient times the stemless thistle was valued by doctors a great deal. An extract prepared from the root or the flower's disc was used for persistent skin rashes, herpes etc. According to some views its scientific generic name is related to Charlemagne, who is said to have advised his soldiers to eat it. Stemless thistle is a perennial plant. It grows from northern Greece and Spain across Europe to western USSR. It forms two types: one is stemless, with leaves in a basal rosette and the second with up to 30 cm tall, leafy stems. The edible part of the flower head is the disc. The flower head is cut off in the beginning of May and the whorl of bracts surrounding the florets and the florets themselves are removed. Its flavour is similar to that of a kohlrabi. It contains a volatile oil, inulin (sugar suitable for diabetics), tannins, resin, saponins and other influential substances. It has considerable antibacterial properties. Since the stemless thistle is on the decrease, the flower heads can only be cut where it grows profusely. In any case the flower head has to be cut off carefully so as not to damage the root in the ground. In some countries stemless thistle is a protected species. The flower discs are eaten raw with pepper and garlic salt or they can be prepared as an hors-d'oeuvre similar to the artichokes.

Description
Stemless thistle (1) is a perennial prickly plant with a sturdy, unbranched rootstock and numerous roots. It grows on dry slopes, along field edges, in clearings and meadows with plenty of sun and in rocky ground. Its stem is usually stunted, so that the flower head is attached directly to the rosette; in the other type it is up to 30 cms tall, leafy and terminates in a single flower head. The leaves in the basal rosette are elongated, spiny-serrated, thorny and tough. The flower heads (2 — cross-section) are up to 15 cm in diameter, and are present from July to September. The outer spiny bracts look like small leaves. The central scaly bracts are brownish and have comb-like thorny margins. The numerous inner bracts are narrow, long, white and yellow on the underside. All the bracts are dry-membranous and open in the sun. When it is damp they close and so protect the flower head from rain (3). The tubular, bisexual florets are white or pinkish. The flower disc produces a white milk when cut. The fruit is small and dry.

Stemless Thistle with Garlic Butter and Cheese

Ingredients
8 flower discs, 200 g grated cheese, 2 tbsp butter, 2 cloves of garlic, salt

Method
Boil the discs in salty water. Melt the butter and stir in the pressed garlic. Sprinkle with cheese and melted butter. Serve with toast and vegetables.

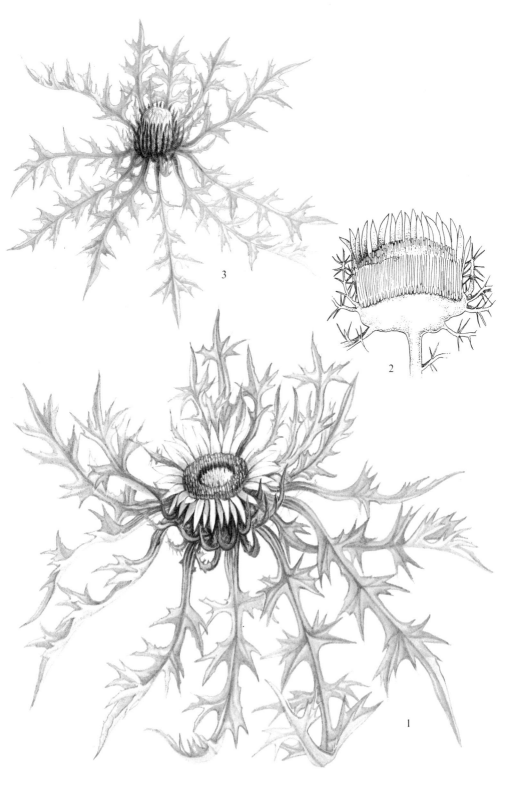

Caraway
Carum carvi

Umbelliferae

Caraway is one of the oldest spices used in Europe. Its fruits were found even in neolithic pile-dwellings. The first written records about the use of caraway come from the time of Charlemagne. It is found growing wild in Europe, the Caucasus, Siberia, central Asia and has been introduced to all continents. Originally the seeds were collected only from wild plants, now caraway is commonly cultivated. Varieties cultivated in central European countries are all popular but the best type is the large-seeded caraway from the Netherlands. Caraway seeds obtained from wild-growing plants have a stronger aroma than that of cultivated types. The flavour and aroma of the seeds are due to a volatile oil (3—7 per cent) with its main components carvone (50—60 per cent) and limonene. They also contain tannins, proteins, fatty oil, sugars, flavonoids and other substances. The leaves have a lesser quantity of volatile oil but in addition they contain carotene and vitamin C. As a result of its high content of carvone the caraway is a reliable carminative agent. It aids digestion and is useful in problems arising from flatulence. It is effective against intestinal colics and provides an essential oil against intestinal parasites. In spring the young leaves are collected before the plant starts to flower. They are used to season herb soups, potato dishes, salads, omelets, sauces and soft cheese spreads. The seeds are collected in July and August. They have a sharp spicy taste and aroma and are used dried, either whole, crushed or ground to season rye bread, cheeses, savoury pastry, mushrooms, roast meats, soups, sauces, cabbage dishes and cakes. They are used in spice mixtures, in food conserving and in the production of liqueurs.

Description

Caraway (1) is a biennial member of the carrot family. In the wild it grows in meadows, pastures, at the edges of fields and roads, mostly in damp, fertile soils from lowlands to higher altitudes. In the first year of its growth it forms a spindle-shaped root and a rosette of basal, stalked leaves, each divided into several leaflets. In the second year an erect, grooved angular, sparsely branched stem develops, reaching a height of up to 1 metre. The stem leaves are smaller than the basal ones and have a stalkless sheath (2). Small white flowers (3), arranged in an umbrella-shaped spray, are present from May to June. These ripen from July to August into small, dry, flat fruits each of which splits from its lower end into two crescent-shaped fine-ribbed seeds. Due to the essential oil contained in canals located between these ribs, the seeds emit a pleasant aroma when rubbed between the fingers.

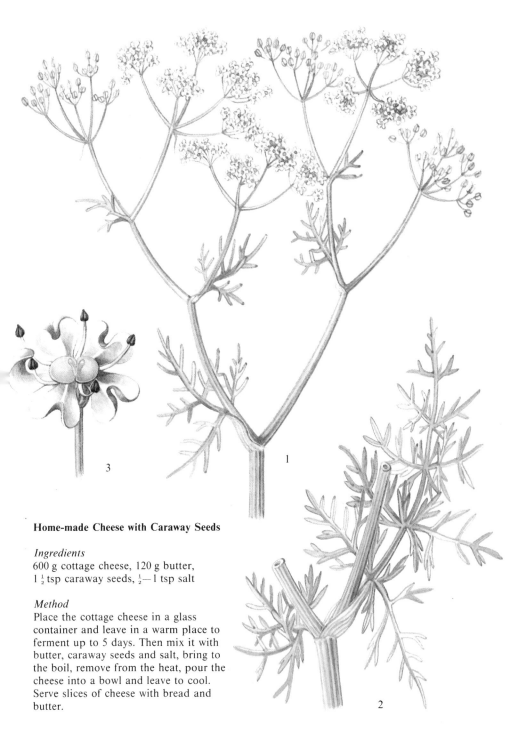

Home-made Cheese with Caraway Seeds

Ingredients
600 g cottage cheese, 120 g butter,
1 ½ tsp caraway seeds, ½—1 tsp salt

Method
Place the cottage cheese in a glass
container and leave in a warm place to
ferment up to 5 days. Then mix it with
butter, caraway seeds and salt, bring to
the boil, remove from the heat, pour the
cheese into a bowl and leave to cool.
Serve slices of cheese with bread and
butter.

Sweet Chestnut
Castanea sativa
Fagaceae

Sweet chestnut originated in Asia Minor, from where it was introduced to Greece and later to southern Italy and Spain. Today it
grows wild around the Mediterranean sea as far as Iran. It is most
common in southern Europe but the fruits will ripen even in the
warmer parts of central Europe. It has been cultivated since ancient
times. It is planted like a fruit tree alongside roads, in gardens and
parks. Edible chestnuts were at one time ground into flour for addition to stuffings. The chestnut tree has long been a favourite of man
—even Bronze Age relics of its wood and fruit are known. Mention is
made of the chestnut in the Capitulary of Charlemagne and a herbal
of the Abbess Hildegarde of Bingen recommended a drink from the
leaves in the treatment of whooping cough. The fruits, the chestnuts
themselves that is, are collected at the end of October or in November
when they fall and are dried. If intended to be kept until spring, they
are stored complete with their cupules, the protective outer skin, in
a shallow layer at a temperature of up to 4 °C. They are packed with
nutrition and energy. Apart from water they contain 35—60 per cent
starch, 6—10 per cent proteins, 15—20 per cent sugar (saccharase),
2—7 per cent fats, about 40 mg vitamin C and 15—16 mg vitamin B_1
in 100 g of pulp. They also contain a relatively large amount of potassium and phosphorus and also tannins in their skin. However, they
lack sodium and are therefore a suitable dietary component for those
suffering from high blood pressure and kidney diseases. They are
also effective in treating diarrhoea. However, in folk medicine the
leaves are more frequently used. In regions of both natural occurrence and cultivation, the sweet chestnut is an important food plant.
The nuts are usually eaten roasted, but they can also be boiled (they
should be partly cut, boiled in water and then peeled) or they can be
ground into flour. Apart from all these uses, it is also an important
contributing factor in the production of honey. Chestnuts can be
turned into a delicious purée or soup or can be added to stuffings to
accompany roast meat and poultry.

1

Description
The sweet chestnut is a medium-sized, undemanding tree with unisexual male and female organs on the same plant. In the wild it is propagated by seeds. It is long-lived and only begins to fruit in about its 20th year. Its wood is very hard, harder than even quality oak wood. The leaves (4) are tough and leathery, with short leaf stalks and serrated edges. The fruits of the sweet chestnut (1) ripen in October. They are usually enclosed in threes in a spiny cup-shaped container of 'cupule' (2, 3— the empty cupule). Wild sweet chestnuts have smaller fruits than the cultivated varieties.

3

Chestnut Purée

Ingredients
$\frac{1}{2}$ kg chestnuts, $\frac{1}{4}$ litre milk, 125 g sugar, sprig of vanilla, $\frac{1}{2}$—1 tbsp rum

Method
Scald chestnuts with boiling water. Peel them and boil in milk with the vanilla and sugar, press or grind them and flavour with rum. Purée can be used as filling for desserts or can be served with whipped cream and fruit compote.

2

4

73

Tuberous-rooted Chervil
Chaerophyllum bulbosum

Umbelliferae

Tuberous-rooted chervil originated in north-western and western Europe, occurs also in the wild in central Europe, western Asia and has been introduced to North America. It may be cultivated in Britain. Tuberous-rooted chervil has only been used for food since the 19th century although not very commonly, the edible parts being its root tubers and leaves. It is cultivated sporadically in Hungary, Germany and Spain. In northern regions, for example in Siberia, it is cultivated for its roots, in the south more for its aromatic tops. The plant can be collected in the wild but does not occur there in great profusion. Swollen root tubers of tuberous-rooted chervil taste like chestnuts and contain up to 35 per cent starch. The tubers are collected in October to November or early in spring and if stored in damp sand for a few weeks, their flavour improves. They are thus best consumed from December to March. They are eaten raw, thinly sliced, with pepper, vinegar, oil and salt or boiled like other more common root vegetables such as potatoes. The young tops, which resemble parsley, may be used in salads or added to soups.

Other wild-growing members of the genus *Chaerophyllum* are not edible and do not form the beet-like swollen roots of the edible variety. Examples are *C. hirsutum,* whose leaves smell of apples when rubbed, and *C. aromaticum,* which smells of carrots. Their leaves do not have as many leaflets as those of *C. bulbosum.* Other related species which are also found in the wild, are *C. femulum* und *C. aureum.*

Description

Tuberous-rooted chervil (1) is a biennial plant growing along the edges of damp forests and thickets, on slopes, close to rivers, in fields, along roadsides and also in vineyards. It it an undemanding plant needing light soil for good, healthy root development. In the first year of its growth it forms the bulbous pale yellow root (2) and a rosette of basal leaves, which are divided into leaflets, resembling those of cow parsley or parsley. The flowering stems occurring in the second year are hollow, rounded and bristly, and may reach a height of one and a half metres. They flower in June and July forming white flowers (3) in dense, compound umbrella-shaped sprays. The fruit (4) is small and dry, without a beak. Tuberous-rooted chervil can best be cultivated from seeds sown in autumn or from small subsidiary tubers. The seeds germinate very slowly and lose their power of germination from the second year.

74

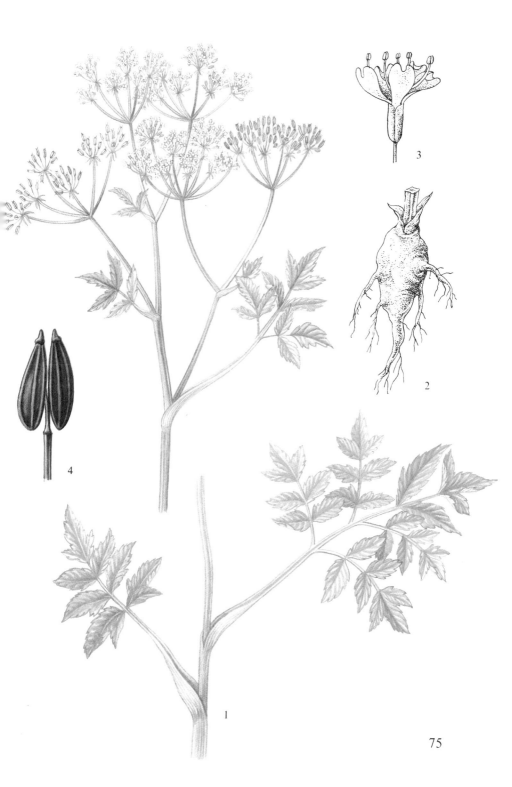

3

2

4

1

75

Fat Hen
Chenopodium album

Chenopodiaceae

The genus *Chenopodium,* which has about 25 species, is the largest in the family Chenopodiaceae. A number of these species were once used extensively as a foodstuff, for example Good King Henry (*C. bonus-henricus*), annual nettle-leaved goosefoot (*C. murale*) and *C. botrys,* originally from southern Europe. However, as a result of the cultivation of leaf vegetables, these wild-growing plants were replaced in the kitchen by the more agreeably tasting spinach and Swiss chard, although the biological value of wild spinach is greater. Fat hen is a common weed in Europe. It grows everywhere, particularly close to human habitation. In central Europe up to 50 per cent of all weed seeds present in the soil are those of fat hen. Its young leaves and juicy stem tops are used for food. When chopped they can be added to soups, stuffings, minced meats, potato dishes etc. They contain more than 14 per cent of dry matter, about 4 per cent proteins and 7 per cent saccharides. In terms of minerals fat hen is highest in calcium and magnesium, but also contains phosphorus and iron. It is also rich in vitamin C, containing as much as 245 mg per 100 g of leaves. The leaves, roots and tops are used in folk medicine to treat coughs and bronchitis, and as a supportive medicine in tuberculosis. It may also be used to treat external wounds.

Description
Fat hen (1) is a tall weed with a tough, branching root. It grows in fields and gardens, on wasteland, compost heaps and close to dung hills. Plants for cooking should not be collected in areas where there is an excessive concentration of nitrogen. The stems have a rich covering of leaves and may be branched if supplied well with nutrients. They may reach a height of one metre. The leaves (2) are ovate, wedge-shaped and irregularly toothed. When young the entire plant is covered with spherical outgrowths giving it the appearance of being covered with flour. Its small greenish flowers (3) occur in densely crowded clusters of flowers along central stems. The fruit (4) is small and dry, containing glossy edible

1

2

black seeds. One plant can produce as
many as a hundred thousand fruits. The
Fat hen is a much variable species
forming many types with different
requirements in terms of locality.

Cornelian Cherry
Cornus mas
Cornaceae

The cornelian cherry grows wild in southern Europe, in the foothills of the Caucasus, in Turkey and in the warmer regions of central Europe. It is rarely seen in the wild in Britain, but may be cultivated. Its fruits, which ripen in August and September, have a reddish, sometimes yellowish juicy flesh with an oval stone inside and a slightly sour, acrid taste. Along with woodland strawberries and raspberries, they have been used since ancient times in the making of preserves and as a medicine. They are high in vitamin C, containing as much as 300 mg vitamin C per 100 g of pulp. The vitamin C content is maintained in products made from the cornelian cherry. Compotes and jams contain 30—50 mg per 100 g, which is more than in raw lemons. Furthermore, cornelian cherries contain sugars, malic and tartaric acids, pectins, tannins, many minerals, especially calcium and magnesium, provitamin A and rutin. The kernel contains as much as 34 per cent oil. In the past, folk medicine recommended the kernel in the treatment of stomach diseases and diarrhoea. In fact, in some countries the fresh juice is still used to treat diarrhoea in children. The bark of the cornelian cherry was formerly used as a yellow home dye. The fruits are collected at the end of September, when fully ripe, before they become too soft. They can be used fresh or dried in the preparation of vitaminized tea, juices, wines, syrups, liqueurs and jams. They can be combined with rowanberries, cranberries and bilberries to make a delicious compote to accompany game. The pith of the fruit eaten with honey is excellent. In the Caucasus dried cornelian cherries are ground to powder for sprinkling on grilled meats or to spice sauces.

3

Description
Cornelian cherry (1) is a shrub or tree growing to a height of 3—7 metres. It grows in calcareous, slightly alkaline soils in dry conditions, usually in clearings, thickets, on rocky slopes and in light woodland. It has opposite, broadly oval, pointed leaves with distinct veins. It is conspicuous by its yellow flowers which open early in spring, often in March and April, before the leaves develop. The flowers (2, 3) occur in umbrella-shaped clusters on a short stalk. They are bisexual, very small with four golden-yellow petals and

similarly coloured stamens. It is very
decorative when in flower, and is
therefore often planted in parks. The
fruit is red, ovoid and contains a stone.
The cornelian cherry is resistant to frost;
its wood does not freeze even in
temperatures of −30 °C.

Powder from Dried Cornelian Cherries

Ingredients
1 kg fresh fruits

Method
Wash the fruits, remove stones and dry.
Grind the dried fruits and store the
powder in a dry, dark place in screw-top
glass jars. The powder has a slightly
sour taste and can be used in flavouring
sauces, soups, salads and sprinkled over
grilled meats.

2

1

79

European Hazel
Corylus avellana
Betulaceae

Neolithic man enjoyed eating hazel-nuts as numerous finds of crushed shells in their pile dwellings testify. Large hazel-nuts were also found in Pompeii and Charlemagne is known to have spread the hazel throughout Europe. The hazel is a much varied species and is native to Europe, Crimea, the Caucasus and Asia Minor. Its cultivated varieties have been developed by the hybridisation of various species. Out of about 15 related species, all of which bear edible nuts, the most frequently encountered are the giant hazel (*C. maxima*) and the Turkish hazel (*C. colurna*). Today the largest amounts of hazels are cultivated in Turkey, in the USSR around the Black Sea, also in Italy, France, England and Sweden. The nuts are picked when they fall out of their cups. After shelling, the kernels are dried in an airy place, the unripe kernels shrivelling significantly. The kernels of hazel-nuts have a high content of nutritious substances as well as a high energy value. Because of their delicate flavour they are more popular than walnuts. They contain about 60 per cent fats, 14—20 per cent proteins, 5 per cent water, 8—14 per cent saccharides, a considerable amount of potassium, phosphorus, calcium, magnesium, iron and copper, along with folic acid, vitamins of the B group, provitamin A, vitamin E and up to 30 mg vitamin C in 100 g. They also have medicinal properties. Grated with honey they are recommended for coughs. They are used mainly in the preparation of desserts, chocolate, petit fours, sauces and icecream. They can also be added to fruit salads and savoury dishes, for example stuffings, soufflés and roast meat.

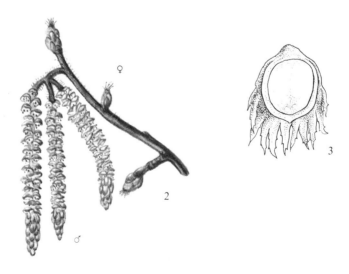

1

Description

European hazel (1) is a shrub or a small tree with grey-brown bark and deciduous leaves. It prefers slightly damp places and is not very demanding in terms of soil. It grows in meadows, at the edges of forests, on slopes or is cultivated in gardens, often being planted to cover barren and neglected locations. It has a soft, flexible wood which is valued by basket makers, woodcarvers and charcoal markers. In spring it is the first tree species to flower and is therefore most useful to bee-keepers. Hazel has long, oval, stalked leaves with serrated edges and downy, especially on their undersides. It is unisexual, the male flowers appearing early in spring in hanging catkins, whilst the female flowers are crowded in bud-like floral arrangements with protruding red stigmas (2). The fruit is a nut enclosed in a leafy cup and a cinnamon brown, hard and smooth shell (3 — longitudinal section).

Midland Hawthorn
Crataegus laevigata
Rosaceae

Hawthorn is a native of Europe, western Asia and also north-western Africa. The first records of its use date from the beginning of our era from Dioscorides. There is on record a recipe dating from about 1000 AD for the Frankish kings, for a syrup made from the fruit to counteract ageing. Later on the interest in hawthorn subsided and was only revived again at the end of the 19th century. The unopened buds are edible and have a fine, nut-like flavour. When fresh and finely chopped, they can be added to potato or lettuce salads, soft cheese spreads etc. The fruits are picked in the autumn and are at their best after the first frost, when they are fully ripe. They taste floury, slightly sour or bitter, but after freezing their flavour improves and from them we can prepare syrups, or when dried, a medicinal tea. The buds, fruits and also the flowers or leaves with flowers have a considerable medicinal value. They contain a number of flavonoides, amines, choline, organic acids, saponins, sorbitol, pigments, vitamin C and B, purines and catecholic tannins and are effective in the widening of arteries, lowering blood pressure, stimulating heart activity and also acting as a heart sedative.

Description
Six or seven wild species of hawthorn grow in Europe, the best known of which are midland hawthorn (1) and common hawthorn (*C. monogyna*). They

3

grow in thickets on sunny slopes, at the edges of fields, pastures, forests in low-lying warm situations and in the Alps up to altitudes of 1500 metres. Hawthorns grow as thorny bushes or small trees with sharp thorns. The buds (2) are collected early in spring. The alternate, short-stalked leaves have 3—5 lobes with pointed tips and finely serrated edges in midland hawthorn and up to seven blunt, more deeply cut lobes with almost entire margins in common hawthorn. The flowers, opening in May and June, form clusters with a characteristic smell. They have five white or pink petals with numerous stamens and red stigmas. The fruits (3) ripen in the autumn. They are red, floury and cored, bearing remnants of the persistent calyx, or whorl of leaves which formed the outer case of the flower.

Potato Salad with Hawthorn Buds

Ingredients
600 g boiled potatoes, 2 red onions,
3 hard-boiled eggs, $\frac{1}{2}$ l hawthorn buds,
4 tbsp mayonnaise, 2 tbsp plain yoghurt,
1 tbsp white wine, salt, ground pepper,
mustard

Method
Dice boiled potatoes and eggs and cut
onion in rings. Finely chop cleaned buds
of hawthorn. Mix with mayonnaise,
yoghurt and wine, season with salt,
pepper, and if liked, mustard. Chill the
salad and serve as an hors d'oeuvre or
a side dish to accompany meat, hard
boiled eggs, ham etc.

1

2

83

Quince
Cydonia oblonga
Rosaceae

Quince is an old fruit species with a worldwide distribution with its origins in the Caucasus, Iran and Turkestan. It was one of the most highly valued and most popular medicinal plants to be used in ancient times. The Greeks dedicated it to the goddess Aphroditi and in the Middle Ages it was cultivated in monasteries and manorial gardens. The Greeks and Romans began its cultivation in Europe and as early as the time of Pliny the Elder six species were known. It has undergone renewed popularity recently due to its healthy properties and in some countries its cultivation has been increased. In Switzerland, France, Italy and Moldavia large orchards are in existence. The quince may be cultivated in Britain. The fruits of the quince are picked at the end of October. They cannot be eaten straightaway and must be allowed to mellow. Products made from them are delicious and healthy. The pulp of the quince is hard and has an astringent taste. It contains up to 14 per cent sugar (mainly glucose and fructose), organic acids (malic, tartaric, citric), pectin, tannins, volatile oil, mucilages (present mainly in the seeds), provitamin A, up to 20 mg vitamin C per 100 g pulp, iron, copper, potassium, magnesium, calcium and phosphorus. A pleasantly scented volatile oil is present, mostly in the skin. The quince is effective against diarrhoea, the inflammation of mucous membranes, intestines and stomach. Its seeds, however, are poisonous. Quinces are used for making ciders, compotes, jelly, marmalade and wine. They can be also added to meat dishes. Sliced quinces can be dried moderate temperatures. They are also used in the cosmetic industry and for medicinal cosmetics. The fruits of Japanese quince (*Chaenomeles japonica*), a red flowering ornamental shrub, can be used in the same way as other quinces.

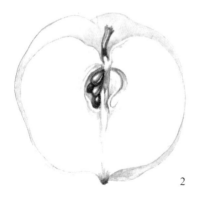

2

Quince Jelly

Ingredients
$\frac{1}{2}$ kg quinces, $\frac{1}{2}$ kg apples, 1 kg sugar, 1 litre water

Method
Peel apples and quinces, boil in water and strain. Add the sugar, continually stir and boil until thick.

1

3

Description
Quince (1) is a warmth-loving shrub or small tree, thriving particularly in apricot and peach growing regions. It has tough, ovate, entire, dark green leaves which are white-felted on the underside. Similarly white-felted are also the young shoots. It flowers late, in the second half of May. The flowers are large, solitary, and white-pink. The regularly produced fruits (2 — longitudinal section) ripen late and are harvested at the end of October. They are apple- or pear-like, felty, yellow and aromatic when ripe. They contain five membranous multi-seeded capsules with 6—16 seeds (3).

Chufa
Cyperus esculentus   Cyperaceae

Chufa, also called tiger nut, is reminiscent of a tuft of grass or sedge. It comes from southern Europe, the Near East and North Africa. It grows wild in the region of the White Nile in Upper Egypt and the Sudan and may be cultivated in Britain. Indeed, it has been cultivated since ancient Egypt. Its root stems were found in the tombs of Egyptian kings dating back to the 3rd and 2nd millenium B.C. Theophrastes mentions this species as an edible grass which grows alongside rivers and whose sweet root stems are boiled in beer. Credit for spreading it belongs to the Arabs who often ate its root stems rather than almonds. Today it is cultivated mostly in Spain and Italy, and also in Hungary, the USA and the south of the European part of the USSR. Since its root stems contain an oil which is very valuable for the food industry, it is being intensively improved to enlarge their size. Chufa in fact is an oil plant. It contains as much as 20 per cent oil, in quality comparable to olive oil, up to 30 per cent starch, 14—15 per cent sugar, up to 10 per cent protein and some vitamins. Its reddish root stems are harvested in October, whole tufts of chufa being pulled out and the root stems picked off and washed. They can be used in a number of ways: boiled as vegetables, eaten raw like almonds or roasted as peanuts. Roasted ground root stems can also be used as a substitute for cocoa and coffee. The flour from the ground root stems can also be added to confectionery. Raw root stems make a nutritious fodder, especially for pigs.

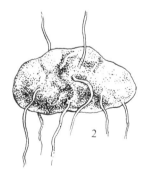

Description
Chufa (1) is a perennial plant, 20—60 cms tall. It requires sufficient moisture and a warm sandy soil. Its leaves have 4 mm wide, long blades. Globular or cask-shaped, 1.5—2 cms long tubers (2) are formed at the end of short projecting underground shoots.

86

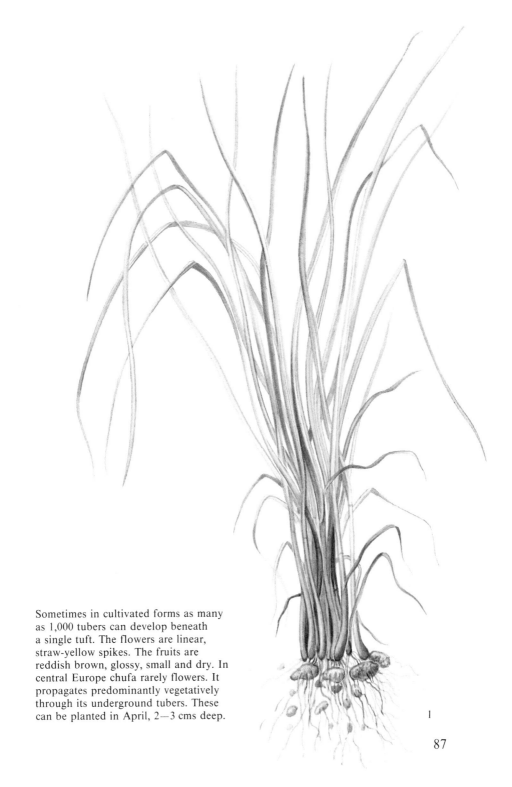

Sometimes in cultivated forms as many
as 1,000 tubers can develop beneath
a single tuft. The flowers are linear,
straw-yellow spikes. The fruits are
reddish brown, glossy, small and dry. In
central Europe chufa rarely flowers. It
propagates predominantly vegetatively
through its underground tubers. These
can be planted in April, 2—3 cms deep.

1

Rose-bay Willow-herb
Epilobium angustifolium
Oenotheraceae

In summer large growths of this attractive pink-flowering perennial can be found in light clearings, at the edges of forests, on banks and sunny slopes, in ditches and alongside roads. It is so characteristic that it cannot be confused with any related species. Its flowers are important in honey production and bees can produce as much as 500 kg of light green flavoursome honey from 1 hectare of this flowering weed. Rose-bay willow-herb is widespread particularly in Europe but also in Asia and North America. The young leaves and root stems are edible. The leaves contain tannins, mucilages, pectins, sugars and also a lot of vitamin C. They can be collected throughout the plant's growing season. The root stems have less tannins and mucilages than the leaves and are dug up early in spring or in the autumn. The dried or fermented leaves are used in the preparation of a tea which is popular in eastern Europe and Asia. It has calming effect on the nervous system and is an effective treatment for insomnia and migraine. Its root stems are eaten raw, prepared as a salad or as a compote. They can be also preserved in alcohol.

Description
Rose-bay willow-herb (1) is a robust perennial which grows to a height of one metre. It spreads by its underground creeping root stems (2) with scaly, non-rooting shoots. The root stems produce erect, unbranched densely leafy,

4

often reddish stems. The leaves (3) are
narrow, alternate, spear- to
wedge-shaped and pointed at the tip.
They resemble the leaves of some willow
species and are ash-greyish green on the
underside. The stem terminates in a rich
central-stemmed cluster of flowers and
buds growing out of the axils of linear
stipules. The flowers (4) have red sepals
and bear four purple red, occasionally
white, petals and appear from June to
September. They open gradually from
the lower part of the inflorescence and
new buds continue to develop all the
time at its apex, whilst in the lower part
of the stem the ripe capsules are already
releasing seeds. The seeds are equipped
with woolly pubescence and are easily
carried by the wind.

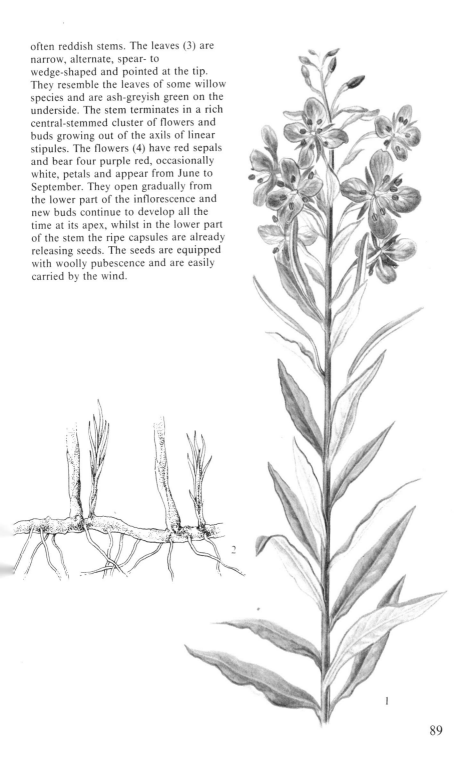

Beech
Fagus sylvatica
Fagaceae

Beech is widespread in southern and western Europe, to the north it reaches southern Sweden and in the east as far as the Crimea. In central Europe it grows mainly in submountain and mountain regions, locally up to a height of 1,300 metres above sea level and in Germany and Poland also along the coastline. At lower altitudes it grows predominantly in association with oaks, and at heights of about 600 metres above sea level it often forms pure growths. At higher altitudes it forms communities with firs, maples and spruces. Beech woods come into leaf relatively late and therefore in early spring a rich spring flora can form under the trees. The fruits, beech nuts, are the part of the tree most usually eaten, however sometimes the buds are consumed. The kernel of the nut contains about 40 per cent oil and its taste is reminiscent of hazel nuts. As late as the First World War oil was being pressed from beech nuts, and the oil pressed by using the cold method is indeed very tasty. Eating ripe dried or roasted beech nuts is an ancient Slav practice. However, beech nuts do contain some harmful substances, namely fagin and oxalic acid. However, these substances remain in the solid remnants during the pressing process and are not transferred to the oil. In addition to fats the beech nuts contain about 23 per cent protein, 22 per cent saccharides and 3.5 per cent minerals, particularly calcium, phosphorus and magnesium but also iron and vitamins of the B group. Semi-opened buds are used in England to make a home liqueur. The buds can be preserved in gin, after steeping, sugar being added to the liquid.

Description
Beech (1) has characteristic long, pointed buds. The leaves are as if pleated in the bud, later having broad oval, wavy-edged serrated or finely toothed blades with conspicuous veins (2). The beech flowers at the same time as the leaves bud in April and May. The male flowers are on long stalks in hanging compact terminal clusters, whilst the female flowers always develop in twos and are enclosed in a spiny

3

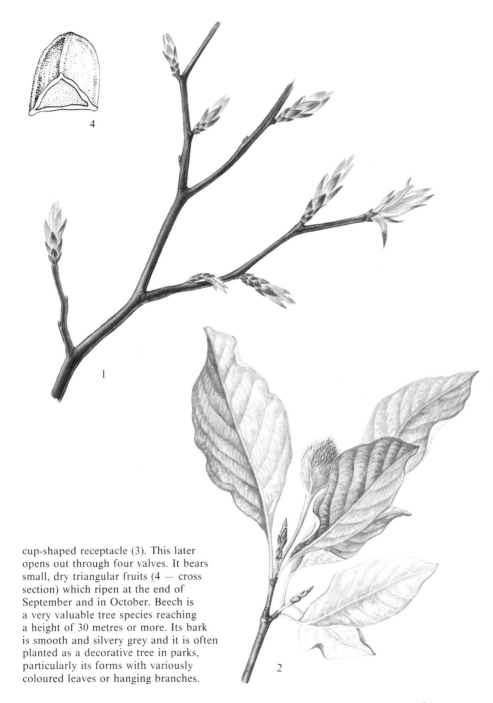

4

1

cup-shaped receptacle (3). This later
opens out through four valves. It bears
small, dry triangular fruits (4 — cross
section) which ripen at the end of
September and in October. Beech is
a very valuable tree species reaching
a height of 30 metres or more. Its bark
is smooth and silvery grey and it is often
planted as a decorative tree in parks,
particularly its forms with variously
coloured leaves or hanging branches.

2

Hautbois Strawberry
Fragaria moschata
Rosaceae

Hautbois strawberry is found primarily in central Europe. It was in the past introduced in Britain but is now rarely seen in the wild; it can, however, be cultivated. The hautbois strawberry is not as common as the wild strawberry (*F. vesca*). It grows in grassy places from the lowlands to the foot of mountains and can be found in sparse woods, thickets, clearings, meadows, on pastureland, slopes, and in parks. Both fruits and leaves are collected, the fruits having similar medicinal effects to those of wild strawberry. They contain about 30 mg vitamin C per 100 g of pulp, carotene, vitamins B and K, sugars, fruit acids (above all citric), fibres, tannins, volatile oils, salicylic and silicic acids and other substances. In terms of minerals they contain iron, phosphorus, calcium, sodium and sulphur. The strawberries, which have a characteristic musk-like aroma, are made into jams, compotes, syrups etc., used for dessert fillings and fruit soups. The leaves also have medicinal properties. Tea made from its leaves is recommended for abdominal and intestinal catarrhs, kidney and urinary tract diseases.

Description
Hautbois strawberry (1) is taller than wild strawberry, reaching a height of 40 cms. It forms a perennial rootstock in the ground. Its runners are shorter, sometimes missing altogether so that it does not spread vegetatively very quickly. The leaves are three-parted, with short leaf stalks. The flowering stems terminate in a rich cluster of flowers and considerably extend above the leaves of the basal rosette. The flowers (2) are large, white, borne on downy stalks. They appear in May and June. The fruit (3) is a globe- to pear-shaped berry with small dry fruits on the surface, or more precisely, an aggregate fruit on a fleshy receptacle. The ripe berry is aromatic, often asymmetrical, greenish white, with a reddish hue on the side turned to the sun. It is difficult to separate it from its downy calyx.

Sweet Strawberry Soup

Ingredients
500 g fresh strawberries, 100 g castor sugar, several sponge biscuits, ½ glass of cream

Method
Wash and liquidize strawberries. Boil sugar in 1 litre water to make a syrup, allow to cool and mix with fruit pulp and cream. Place several sponge biscuits in every portion of soup.

2

1

3

Wood Strawberry
Fragaria vesca

Rosaceae

Wood strawberry is widespread throughout the whole of Europe, growing in forests, clearings, on slopes and close to roads from lowlands to mountains. It is found in Asia as far as Baikal and partly as a native but also introduced to North America and Australia. Europe is the home of two related species, the hautbois strawberry and the wild strawberry. Wood strawberry is, however, the most common, its scientific name being derived from the Latin word *fragrans,* which means aromatic. The fruits, which ripen in June and July, are a nutritious and healthy delicacy. They contain 80—90 per cent water, 6 per cent sugar, 1 per cent protein, the malic and citric organic acids, essential oils, cellulose, pectins, tannins and considerable amounts of iron, calcium, phosphorus and potassium. Its iodine content is also very valuable, 100 g of strawberries containing up to 100 mg of vitamin C, also 0.1 mg vitamin B and K. Strawberries slightly reduce fever, improve digestion and have a beneficial effect on the blood pressure. Their iron content promotes the formation of blood and they also have a diuretic effect. However, in some people they cause an allergic rash, and if so they should be complemented by cottage cheese or honey. Strawberries are made into jams, compotes, marmalades, juices, syrups, wines and liqueurs. They can be also frozen or dried and added to various tea mixtures. The fruits of wood strawberry also have cosmetic effects on the skin. The young leaves also have medicinal properties. They can be used fresh in a mixture of other herbs for soups or dried, and sometimes fermented (description on p. 96) for the preparation of tea which is then drunk to treat kidney inflammation, to aid the metabolism and calm the nervous system or used as a gargle and in medicinal cosmetics.

2

Description
Wood strawberry (1) is a perennial, 10—30 cms tall herb with composite three-parted leaves and with a long, hairy stalk. The individual leaflets (2) are oval, coarsely serrated, shiny and downy beneath. The flowers which appear from April to August are white, five-petalled, on a stalk almost as long as the leaf stalk. The fruit (3) is a red berry which in fact is a fleshy receptacle

3

covered with small, dry yellow seeds.
The ripe berry easily becomes detached
from the calyx which has erect sepals
unlike other woodland strawberries. It
propagates vegetatively, forming
numerous shoots on the rooting runners.
It quickly overgrows open sunny
locations. Cultivated varieties came into
existence by crossing and improving
wild strawberries. They yield large fruits
but their leaves are not used.

1

Wild Strawberry
Fragaria viridis

This is another wild strawberry species, occurring in Europe and Asia. It grows in sparse oak forests and grassy thickets, on sunny slopes and dry meadows. It is not very common but where it does occur, it forms extensive growths where conditions are convenient, particularly where there is sufficient sunshine. Both fruits and leaves are used in a similar way to the wood strawberry, the fruits being consumed raw, the leaves added to soups and dried to make tea. Only young leaves should be collected, during the flowering season or even later as the new leaves keep growing during the summer. The fruits contain 20—50 mg vitamin C per 100 g of pulp, vitamins of the B group, also vitamin K, carotene, sugars, organic acids such as salicylic acid, tannins and volatile oils. They are a source of a number of minerals, above all iron, calcium, potassium and phosphorus. The fresh leaves have 150—200 mg vitamin C per 100 g — even more than parsley. They are added fresh, finely chopped, to soups *after* boiling in order to conserve their vitamin C content. They can also be dried for tea, however for this purpose the fermented leaves are tastier. The wilting leaves are crushed with a rolling pin, wrapped firmly in a tea towel and left for about 36 hours. The leaves become darker and develop a more intensive aroma. They can then be dried and kept in a dry place.

Description
Wild strawberry (1) grows to a height of 5—30 cms. The flowering stems are slightly taller than the leaves and the creeping runners are short or absent altogether. The leaves are three-parted on long stalks, the individual leaflets (2) being hairy with serrately toothed edges. The flowers, occurring in May and June, are yellowish white and relatively large. The fruits ripen in June—July, with the calyx pressed to the berry, and remaining attached to it. The ripe berry (3) is greenish white with a faint reddish tinge.

Wild Strawberry Leaf Tea

Method
Scald 1—2 tbsp dried leaves with a glass
of boiling water. The tea can be drunk
every day as a substitute for real tea. It
has a slight anti-inflammatory effect in
treating intestinal catarrh, kidney
troubles and diseases of the urinary
tract.

97

Sweet Woodruff
Galium odoratum
Rubiaceae

Sweet woodruff has been a popular medicinal and culinary herb ever since the Middle Ages. The Benedictine monks used to make 'May wine', an aromatic drink made of white wine spiced with sweet woodruff. However, this beverage was not quite harmless to health since the coumarin glycoside contained in the plant has slight toxic effects, causing headaches, drowsiness and dizziness. The tops of the sweet woodruff are collected at the beginning of the flowering period, when the characteristic aroma is at its strongest. The content of effective substances is highest in spring, reducing by one sixth towards autumn. Apart from the coumarin glycoside, which releases coumarin during drying, sweet woodruff contains organic acids, tannins, bitter principles, vitamin C, essential oils and nicotinamide. The plant smells pleasantly of coumarin and has a slightly bitter taste. It has medicinal properties, due to its anti-spasmodic effects it can be used to treat stomach aches and flatulence. It is also effective in the treatment of insomnia and nervous irritation since it has a general calming effect. It acts also as a mild diuretic. However, because of its slight toxic effects it can only be used from time to time and in small quantities. The fresh and dried tops are used to aromatize wine and liqueurs, milk, puddings, cider, fruit soups, sauces and even smoked meats. It is used in the preparation of drinks by steeping its shoots for several hours in liquid. Apart from this it is also used to aromatize stored clothes and tobacco products.

3

Sweet Woodruff Tea

Ingredients
1 part each of dried leaves of strawberry, blackberry, nettle, tops of balm and sweet woodruff

Method
Scald 1 tbsp of the herbal mixture with a glass of boiling water and allow to stand for 15 minutes. Strain the tea and drink it in the morning and in the evening always at a week's interval. Sweet woodruff tea has a general overall calming effect.

Description

Sweet woodruff (1) is a Eurasian species, most common in the lowland and mountainous regions of central and northern Europe and has also been introduced to North America. It grows mainly in oak, beech and hornbeam forests where it forms a part of the herbaceous cover. It is a perennial with slender, creeping root stems, rhizomes and square, erect stems reaching a height of up to 30 cms. The leaves (2) are arranged in whorls of eight, and are spear-shaped with rough edges. The small flowers (3) are white in colour and form cymose clusters which open from May to June and have a pleasant aroma. The fruit is a small, dry globe-shaped double seed pod densely covered with hooked bristles.

2

1

Wood Avens, Herb Bennet
Geum urbanum
Rosaceae

Wood avens was a well-respected medicinal herb, its use dating from ancient times. Pliny the Elder recommended it as a treatment for diseases of the upper respiratory tract. Its specific name *urbanum* was attributed to it because it grew close to city walls. It is used as a medicinal herb even today but its culinary uses have almost been forgotten. The root stem is dug up in the autumn during November or else very early in spring. The roots and green parts are removed, it is washed, and then dried in the shade. It is used as a substitute for cloves and cinnamon, having a pleasant clove-like aroma and can also be used to make home-made liqueurs and wines. If stored, it must be kept in a dry place. In early spring it is also possible to collect the shoots of young stems, which can then be added to herb soups and sauces. The whole plant, the root and the tops, contain a volatile oil with eugenol, up to 30 per cent tannins, bitter principles and flavonoides; the tops contain vitamin C, provitamin A, saccharides etc. These substances are effective in treating excessive acidity of the stomach, intestinal colics and diarrhoea, and they also improve the appetite. An extract can be used in gargles and for rinsing the mouth to treat bleeding gums and unpleasant breath. Water avens (*G. rivale*) with red flowers has a similar use. Both species crossbreed but water avens does not have as many tannins.

2

Description
Wood avens (1) is a perennial weed. It inhabits the temperate zone of Europe and Asia, also North Africa, North America and Australia. It grows abundantly in gardens, thickets, ditches, in light woodland, wasteland, neglected meadows and other similar places. It thrives at all altitudes. In the ground it has an unbranched rootstock (2) with a clump of firm brown roots. The basal rosette produces several erect, slightly branching, downy stems. The flowers develop individually on long stalks in the axils of the leaves. They are inconspicuous and have five yellow petals with a large number of stamens and pistils. The fruits (3) are small, dry and hairy, with hooked bristles in a spiky head (4).

100

Wild Apple Soup

Ingredients
5—6 wild apples, 50 g dried rose-hips,
100 g sugar, 100 g boiled rice, 50 g
chopped walnuts, root of wood avens

Method
Scald the rosehips with $1\frac{1}{4}$ litres boiling
water and leave to stand for 2 hours.
Strain the liquid, add sugar, cleaned,
chopped root of wood avens, grated
apples and rice. Boil long enough to
tenderize the ingredients and serve hot
with grated walnuts.

1

3

101

Ground-ivy
Glechoma hederacea
Labiatae

Ground-ivy has been used in the kitchen since ancient times. It can be found almost anywhere in the countryside and is widespread in the whole of Europe, northern Asia, even reaching Japan. It is an excellent component of spring herb soups and salads. The young juicy shoots at the start of the flowering season and the young leaves can be collected. They are at their tastiest in spring, in April and May, but can be collected until June. They have an aromatic scent and a slightly bitter, spicy taste. As a spice they can be used fresh or dried. The drying must be done very carefully since the plant contains a volatile oil. Dried ground-ivy is kept in tightly closed containers and should be protected from the light. It contains as much as 7 per cent tannins, a volatile oil, a compound of bitter principle called glechonin, choline, organic acids, saponins, minerals and carotenoids. 100 g of fresh shoots contain about 50 mg vitamin C. Ground-ivy is used to season vegetable and meat stews, forcemeats, potato and vegetable soups. The fresh tops are used to flavour omelets, herb butters, cottage cheese and cheese spreads, scrambled eggs, potato salads, boiled potatoes, rice and pasta. As a medicinal herb it improves the digestion and appetite and is recommended in the treatment of reduced acidity of the stomach.

3

Description
Ground-ivy (1) is a perennial herb reaching a height of 40 cms with rooting shoots up to one metre in length. It grows abundantly in forests, thickets, in clearings, on slopes, alongside roads, and in gardens from lowlands to mountains. The stems are square, hairy and branching. The stalked leaves (2) grow in opposite pairs and have coarsely notched edges. The lower ones are kidney-shaped, those at the top heart-shaped. The flowers (3) are borne at the axils of leaves, are violet-blue, occasionally pink or white, and arranged in groups of two or three with a sparsely hairy surrounding whorl of leaves. The fruits are nutlets. A similar, more robust ivy *G. hirsuta* is not collected since it has an unpleasant smell.

Easter Forcemeat

Ingredients
500 g minced meat, a plateful of nettles,
1 onion, 2—3 cloves of garlic,
2 breadrolls, $\frac{1}{2}$ cup milk, 1 egg, salt,
ground pepper, a pinch of marjoram,
savory and hyssop, 1 tbsp each fresh
chopped chives, parsley and ground-ivy,
50 g bacon, butter

Method
Mix minced meat with scalded, drained,
finely chopped nettles, onion and
crushed garlic. Add cut breadrolls
soaked in milk and squeezed, egg, salt,
spice and herbs. Mix well and shape
into a loaf. Place in a baking tray
greased with butter, place slices of
bacon on top and bake.

1

2

Floating Sweetgrass
Glyceria fluitans

Poaceae

This robust grass, often with its stalks lying in water, can be found in the company of sedges in the shallow waters of ponds, ditches and canals close to the banks. As late as the 19th century the small grains of this aquatic grass were on sale in markets. It was called manna grass, in German *Mannaschwaden,* in French *Herbe à la manne.* The floating sweetgrass grows almost throughout Europe, in the Caucasus, in Morocco, in North and South America. In the past it was a very popular foodplant in Poland, Bohemia, Silesia and east Prussia. In the Ore Mountains in Bohemia it was even being cultivated in the 17th century in drained ponds and other muddy locations for the small yellowish or whitish, elongated grains, similar in shape and flavour to semolina. The spikes are harvested in dew or fog, so that they are not too dry and the grains do not fall out of them. The grains are used in the preparation of a milk pudding, tastier than semolina pudding, or they can be used to thicken soups. Floating sweetgrass is eaten by animals because its spikes and stalks are relatively soft and easily digestible even in late summer.

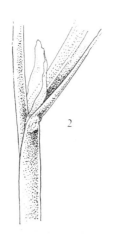

Description
Floating sweetgrass (1) is a bluish green grass with ascending or creeping stems 40—100 cms tall. The leaves have closed sheaths and there are membranous projections (2) between the sheath and the leaf blade. The stem terminates in a one-sided oat-like spray of spikelets. The grass flowers from May to August and the grains do not ripen evenly. They are harvested in August and September. Floating sweetgrass becomes rooted in accumulated dead vegetation in open waters; as a result of regulating the level of the water table, irrigation and land improvement, this perennial acquatic grass is slowly disappearing from the countryside. On the banks of water bodies it is possible to find some related species, for example *G. aquatica,* which reaches a height of $2\frac{1}{2}$ metres with broad blades and branched oat-like sprays and also *G. plicata,* which reaches a height of 1 metre with a spreading oat-like interrupted spray. However, their grains are not collected for food.

1

105

Gooseberry
Grossularia uva-crispa

Grossulariaceae

Gooseberry, an original European species, started to be cultivated as early as the 11th century in Russian monasteries. In western Europe it has been cultivated since the 16th century. It quickly spread to European gardens and this gave rise to many cultivars. Wild gooseberry grows in Europe, Central Asia and North America. Two wild subspecies can be found growing in Europe, namely *G. uva-crispa lasiocarpum* with downy fruits and glossy leaves and *G. u.-c.* ssp. *uva-crispa* with smooth fruits and dull leaves. In North America other wild species occur, which were used in cross-breeding to produce the modern cultivated varieties and make them more resistant to diseases caused by ascomycetous fungi. The fruits of the Gooseberry are collected as early as June. In the sun they ripen earlier, in the shade later. They are small, hairy to bristly berries, relatively sweet, with numerous seeds. They contain saccharides, particularly glucose and fructose, cellulose, pectin—which is why gooseberry jam sets well—and of the organic acids mainly citric acid. The content of provitamin A is considerable, being five times greater than in orange juice. They also contain about 50 mg vitamin C per 100 g of pulp and in terms of mineral substances mostly potassium, phosphorus, calcium, iron, copper, sodium and magnesium. The ripe fruits can be eaten raw; their skin is difficult do digest and must be chewed well. Gooseberries have diuretic and laxative effects. They can be made into marmalades, jams, jellies, compotes, juices, often mixed with other fruits such as strawberries or cherries. Gooseberries are also used to make warm and cold soups and sauces to accompany meat.

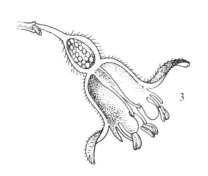

Description
Wild gooseberries (1) are characterized by their shrub-like appearance and the conspicuous sharp thorns (2) on their shoots. The gooseberry is a plant occurring in sparse, mainly deciduous forests at medium to high altitudes where there is sufficient moisture in the air. It is also common on slopes, rocks or in thickets and hedges. The shrubs bud early in spring and the leaves have 3—5 lobes, are either glossy or dull green. The flowers (3—longitudinal section) have short stalks and are rarely single, usually growing in clusters of

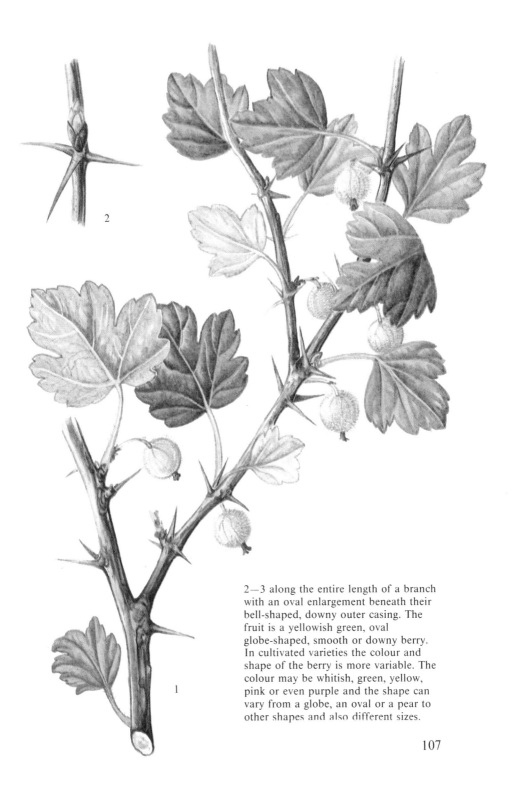

2—3 along the entire length of a branch with an oval enlargement beneath their bell-shaped, downy outer casing. The fruit is a yellowish green, oval globe-shaped, smooth or downy berry. In cultivated varieties the colour and shape of the berry is more variable. The colour may be whitish, green, yellow, pink or even purple and the shape can vary from a globe, an oval or a pear to other shapes and also different sizes.

Cow Parsnip, Hogweed
Heracleum sphondylium
Umbelliferae

This well-known plant, considerably varied in the shape of its leaves, has a very characteristic overall shape and a typical, not very pleasant odour. The young budding leaves and shoots can be used as a side dish or mixed with other herbs, for they can be prepared in the same way as spinach or added to soups. At one time in Russia cow parsnip was added to borshch. In some countries calming liqueur used to improve digestion is still prepared from seeds preserved in spirit. Cow parsnip contains saccharides, proteins, minerals and aromatic substances and is high in vitamin C. However, it is a photodynamic plant, containing photosensibilizing furocoumarins which, if they come into contact with skin or mucous membranes, which are then exposed to the sun, serious inflammations can occur. Cow parsnip is also an old medicinal plant. It regulates the digestion, is mildly laxative and has calming effects. This plant is also good as fodder for farm animals, mainly rabbits.

2

Description
Cow parsnip (1) is a biennial, robust plant which smells unpleasant when rubbed between the fingers. It grows in damp locations from lowland to submountain elevations, in forests and meadows and also on wasteland and in gardens. It is one of the most obstinate and dangerous meadow weeds. In soils fertilized with liquid manure it forms particularly robust individuals which dominate smaller plants. Its stems are erect, hollow, grooved, bristly and up to 150 cm tall. The leaves are large, conspicuous and hairy and vary considerably in shape. The lower leaves (2) have grooved stalks while the upper leaves are sessile with large sheaths. The flowers, which are white, yellow or pink, are arranged in large compound umbrella-shaped clusters at the ends of branches. They appear from May to October, or sometimes later. Cow parsnip bears a small dry double fruit (3) with a broadly winged margin.

Lentils with Barley and Herbs

Ingredients
200 g lentils, 200 g barley, a dish of fresh
herbs (cow parsnip, goutweed, nettles,
orache, fat hen), 100 g bacon, 1 tbsp
vegetable oil, 1 onion, salt

Method
Soak lentils and barley separately for 3
hours and then cook. Chop onion finely
and fry briefly in vegetable oil, add
washed, drained and chopped herbs and
cook for 10 minutes stirring
continuously. Add lentils and barley and
heat through. Serve with gherkins or
sauerkraut.

1

3

Sea Buckthorn
Hippophaë rhamnoides

Elaeagnaceae

Sea buckthorn is distributed throughout the temperate zone or Eurasia. It is quite undemanding with regard to nutrients and moisture and tolerates frosts well. Its fruits are very rich in vitamins, and recently an increased emphasis has been placed on its cultivation and improvement. It is also a very attractive plant, especially in the autumn. The fruits, which have a pineapple-like aroma, are collected when they start to ripen in August and September, while still firm. They are very juicy and sour, and difficult to pick from the thorny branches. They do, however, contain many valuable substances, 100 g of pulp yielding as much as 10 mg provitamin A (this represents 100—200 daily doses for an adult), 900—1,500 mg vitamin C, about 160 mg vitamin E and also vitamins B_1 and B_2. The vitamin content is at its highest in September, but on rainy days this amount is reduced. The fruits also contain many flavonoids, especially rutin, 3—8 per cent oil, fatty acids, sugars, malic and tartaric acids, tannins, volatile oils, potassium, iron, boron and manganese. They can be used to make juices, syrups, jams, marmalades and compotes, and can also be dried. Like cranberries, they can be made into a sauce which goes well with game and grilled meats. Their juice can also be used in place of lemon juice. Mixed with sugar and diluted with water, it makes a refreshing drink to combat fatigue. When processing the fruit it is necessary to take care not to leave the fresh juice exposed to the air for too long, nor to allow it to come into contact with metals or heat it for a long time at a high temperature. Products from sea buckthorn are very important in the treatment of hypovitaminosis, infectious diseases and during convalescence.

Description

Sea buckthorn (1) is a thorny shrub with long underground suckers and dense, spreading, silver-grey branches. It grows on dry, sunny and rocky soils and forms continuous growths up to a height of 2 metres. The alternate leaves (2) are narrow and spear-shaped, smooth on top and silvery felted beneath. The flowers appear in April and May, before the leaves. It is a dioecious shrub, forming separate male and female plants. The antheral flowers are crowded in short catkins: the pistillate form short, sparse clusters. It bears yellow to orange juicy berries (3), densely crowded on branches and ripening from August to October. They have a high biological value and as a result the sea buckthorn is being cultivated to produce large-fruited, thornless varieties. It is also grown in parks and gardens as an ornamental shrub.

2

3

1

111

Hop
Humulus lupulus
Cannabaceae

The hop is native to Europe and western Asia. Both male and female plants can be found growing in the wild in damp locations, coastal thickets and often in alder colonies throughout the whole temperate zone of the northern hemisphere. Their stems, which are several metres long, climb the surrounding trees and shrubs in a clockwise direction. In ancient times it was used both as a medicinal plant and as a vegetable and has a long history of cultivation. The first mention of the cultivation of the hop comes from the records of the Frankish king Pipin the Short, and dates from the 8th century. At that time it was cultivated in monasteries for use in beer making. The female plants form cones, which are an important ingredient in the production of beer; however, they must not be pollinated. It is for this reason that the male wild hop plants in the vicinity of hop fields are destroyed. The hop is what gives the beer its bitterish taste and aroma and helps to preserve it. Hops may also be eaten. The young, soft shoots, prepared as a salad with salt, pepper, vinegar and oil, were already eaten by gourmets during the time of Pliny the Elder. The Italian 16th-century herbalist Pier Andrea Mattioli mentions the young shoots of hops being eaten in the same way as lettuce or asparagus. In hop-growing regions today the young whitish shoots, which have not reached the light, are prepared as asparagus. Early in spring they are separated from the root and eaten raw or boiled. They contain many vitamins of the B group as well as minerals. They are added to salads and omelets; they can be prepared as a side dish with cream sauce or made into a soup. They can be also pickled in vinegar. The hop is an ancient medicinal plant containing bitter principles, resins, volatile oils, tannins and some components with sedative and diuretic effects and an ability to increase the appetite.

Description
The hop (1) is perennial with separate male and female plants annually producing stems up to ten metres in length which bear opposite, palm-shaped leaves with a heart-shaped base. Only the roots overwinter and early in spring they produce new shoots. The stems are covered with hard, hooked hairs, so that they are very rough. The male flowers are arranged in oat-like sprays and have five greenish or

pale yellow petals and five stamens. The
female flowers are short spikelets which
mature into hanging glandular, light
green cones. The glands in female
flower heads contain bitter substances,
of which lupulin is especially effective
in treating nervous irritation. Effective
substances obtained from Hop are also
used in cosmetics.

2

1

Hyssop
Hyssopus officinalis   Labiatae

Hyssop has been a well-known medicinal plant and a spice since ancient times. It reached central Europe in the 9th century from the Mediterranean and Near East where it grows wild. In the Middle Ages it was grown in monasterial and village gardens and was used both as a spice and an expectorant medicine. The plant tops are cut off when the plant begins to flower, are dried in the shade and the dried leaves are shredded. They have a pleasant spicy aroma and bitterish taste and are used to season salads, burgers, stuffings, sauces, herb butters, mayonnaise, liqueurs. They can be added to liver dumplings, soups, ragout, game and poultry. It is advisable to use at the most one teaspoon per portion since hyssop is very aromatic. The hyssop is popular above all in Arabic cuisine. It contains a volatile oil (± 1 per cent), glycosides, a relatively large amount of tannins (8 per cent). It has a high vitamin C content; 100 g of fresh tops contain as much as 170 mg, which is four times more than that of lemons. Furthermore, hyssop contains flavonoids, organic acids and minerals, and in folk medicine it has a similar use to that of sage. It is used to treat inflammations of the upper respiratory tract and asthmatic problems; it improves the function of the digestive tract; it limits perspiration, but should not be used in cases of nervous exhaustion.

Description

Hyssop (1) is a perennial, profusely branched herb. In the wild it grows quite profusely on limestone rocks and screes, in particular in hilly and submountainous regions, in the Mediterranean, in the south of the USSR, in the Near East and the Caucasian region. It was introduced to North America. It is cultivated as a spice and a medicinal plant, which is also important in the production of honey. It temporarily reverts to the wild. Tufts of densely leafy, square stems reaching a height of up to 50 cms, grow from a woody rootstock. The leaves (2) are opposite, spear-shaped, with curled edges and surface with glands which secrete volatile oils. The flowers (3) grow in groups of 4—7 in the joints of upper leaves and form unilateral spike-like sprays (4). The outer case of the flower is tubular, the corolla or inner part of the flower is two-lipped and violet. The fruits are nutlets.

Lamb Patties

Ingredients
500 g minced lamb, 2 onions, 4 cloves of garlic, 1 tsp crushed barberry, $\frac{1}{2}$ tsp ginger, a pinch of cinnamon, a pinch of savory, hyssop, marjoram, hot pepper, ground pepper, salt

Method
Mix minced lamb well with finely chopped onion, crushed garlic, spices and salt. Make patties and roast on grill or charcoal. Serve with tkemali sauce (p. 150).

2

3

4

1

Juniper
Juniperus communis   Cupressaceae

Juniper has a long history; its fruits were first found in neolithic pile-dwellings. During the time of Pliny the Elder, in Roman times, it was used to sweep out houses as a precaution against disease. In the Middle Ages its berries were used as a spice and a juniper twig was worn on the hat as a safeguard against disease. Juniper berries are still used as a medicine and spice. Without them there would be no gin, genever, genièvre or a number of other brandies and liqueurs. Juniper grows throughout the whole of the northern hemisphere in Spain, France, Italy and in the Balkans. In southern Europe it is cultivated for its berries, which are harvested in the trees second year. Gloves should be worn when picking them as the plant is prickly. They are dried for quite a long time in the shade in a shallow layer. They contain a very aromatic, complex volatile oil (about 1 per cent) which is similar to turpentine in its composition, up to 30 per cent inverted sugar, the glycoside juniperin, flavonoids, pigments, pectin, resins, waxes, a small amount of vitamin C and organic acids. They have a slightly sweet, distinctly resinous taste and aroma. When used as a spice, half a teaspoonful of berries per person is sufficient. They are used to spice game, lamb, sauerkraut in a ratio of 6—8 berries per 1 kg, dark sauces and roast poultry. Juniper is particularly recommended for use with heavy foods which may cause flatulence, as it aids digestion.

NOTE: People who suffer from kidney inflammations and also pregnant women should avoid it as it irritates the kidneys.

Description

Juniper (1) is an evergreen coniferous shrub or profusely branched small tree growing as an undergrowth in light woods, on rocks, slopes and heaths, especially on limestone substrata and dry soils, and also in mountainous and submountainous meadows. It is common in pastures where cattle spread its seeds by their droppings. It is also often grown in gardens as an ornamental shrub and is a protected species in many countries. Juniper has both male and female plants, the male being conical, the female widely branched. The leaves are needle-like, sharply pointed, with a canal inside containing volatile oil. The fleshy berry-like cones develop from inconspicuous, green female flowers. At first they are green, ripening only in their second year, when their colour changes to bluish black (2). The shrubs bear ripe and unripe fruits simultaneously. The berry contains between one and three elongated, square, light brown seeds with a hard casing (3 — longitudinal section).

116

3

2

1

Apple
Malus sp.
Rosaceae

It is possible to find many apple species and their hybrids in the wild. There are about fifty species worldwide, and about twenty occur in Eurasia. Their fruits have different shapes and sizes and are edible. The wild apples or those which have become wild usually have, in comparison with cultivated varieties, a lower content of sugars, and more organic acids, pectin and vitamins. They are thus more valuable biologically. They are usually used in the making of ciders, juices, syrups and wine. They can be also baked, added to potato dishes etc. In the past they were used instead of onions. Apples are important for human nutrition, particularly when raw. They contain about 1 per cent pectin, which decreases the amount of cholesterol in the blood, also fruit sugars, malic and citric acids, tannins, aromatic principles, mineral substances (in particular potassium and magnesium, and also phosphorus, calcium, iron, sulphur and manganese), fibre and enzymes which aid digestion. The vitamin content is relatively low; vitamin C is present at 5—50 mg in 100 g pulp. Apples have a mild diuretic action. Tea made from apple peelings has a calming effect; it is slightly diuretic and beneficial in the treatment of rheumatism, liver and kidney diseases. In the Far East young healthy leaves are dried for a vitaminized tea (they contain much vitamin C) or a syrup can be made from them.

Duck Roasted with Wild Apples

Ingredients
1 duck, 750 g apples, sprig of mugwort, 100 g raisins, salt, thyme, butter

Method
Stuff the duck with cored and quartered apples mixed with raisins and add a sprig of mugwort. Salt the duck, sprinkle with thyme, add $\frac{1}{2}$ glass of water and roast, basting during cooking with its juices. Dress the roasted duck with baked apples and raisins and serve with rice.

Description
The apple (1) is a shrub or more frequently a tree bearing alternate stalked oval leaves. The regular, five-petalled, white or pinkish flowers (2) are usually in sparse umbrella-shaped groups. The fruit is floury, fleshy and cored, varying in shape, size and colour. In the wild apple trees grow at the edges of woods, on slopes, pastures and in the vicinity of waterways, where it is also possible to find forms of *Malus pumila*, or crab apple, which have reverted to the wild. Occasionally it is possible to come across wild apple trees with small fruits on short on longer stalks, for example *M. pumila* var. *paradisiaca*. The fruit of all apple trees is edible. Present cultivars, the number of which is estimated at a hundred thousand, have been developed by multiple cross-breeding of the crab apple (*M. sylvestris*), a native of the Caucasus.

118

1

2

Balm
Melissa officinalis
Labiatae

Balm is a very old medicinal plant. It became known mainly as a component of 'Carmelite drops', a universal medicine which the Carmelite monks first produced in Prague in about 1611 AD. At present balm is grown all over Europe. The tops and leaves are used as a spice and medicinal drug. They are cut off when the plant first begins to flower at midday in dry weather. When the plant is in full bloom, the leaves no longer have such a pleasant aroma. The tops should be dried quickly in shallow layers in the shade, in an airy room and without being turned. They can then be shredded. They should not be stored for longer than a year, as they can easily become overheated, turn brown and soon begin to decompose. In particular they contain a volatile oil (up to 0.1 per cent), the composition of which depends on the origins of the plant, its size, amount of hairy covering etc. They also contain tannins, flavonoids, waxes, coumarin and vitamins B_1 and B_2; 100 g of fresh leaves contains as much as 7 mg carotene and 150 mg vitamin C. Balm has similar effects to those of the camomile, which can be fully taken advantage of in the kitchen. It is preferable to use fresh leaves, their delicate lemon-like aroma adding an extra dimension to salads, rice and potatoes (use instead of parsley), omelets, milk, cottage cheese and cream dishes, game, soups, mushrooms, sauces, mayonnaise and fish. They can also be used to add a pleasant lemon aroma to wines, liqueurs, vinegars, milk and other beverages. Tea made from balm is not only very refreshing, but has a number of medicinal properties. It improves the appetite and is effective for treating flatulence and spasms. It slows down the heartbeat and lowers blood pressure and is an effective remedy for palpitations and insomnia. Tea made from balm at a strength of 1 tbsp of the herb per cup of boiling water is recommended before going to sleep. In cosmetics balm is used in a skin mask treatment, hair preparations and skin shampoos. It is also said that its aroma helps to reduce the pain of headaches.

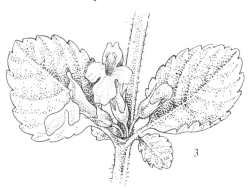

3

Description

Balm (1) is a perennial herb which grows to a height of one metre. It is native to the eastern Mediterranean. In central Europe it has been cultivated since the Middle Ages. The profusely leafy, branched, square stems (2 — cross-section) grow from a scaly root

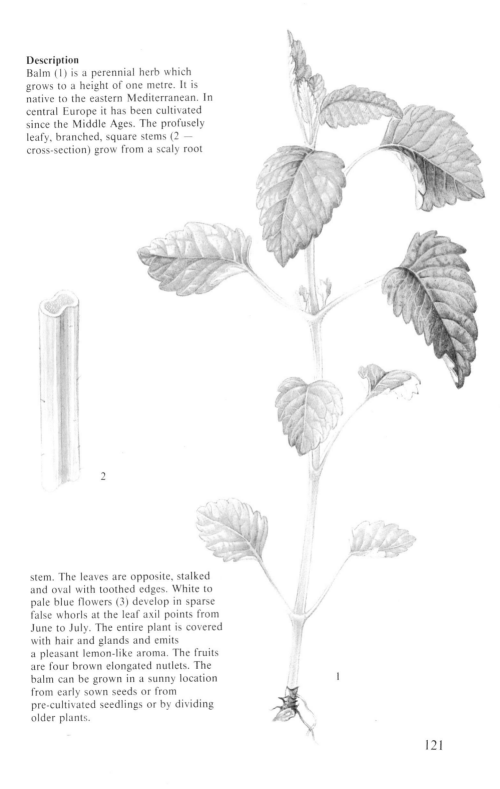

2

stem. The leaves are opposite, stalked and oval with toothed edges. White to pale blue flowers (3) develop in sparse false whorls at the leaf axil points from June to July. The entire plant is covered with hair and glands and emits a pleasant lemon-like aroma. The fruits are four brown elongated nutlets. The balm can be grown in a sunny location from early sown seeds or from pre-cultivated seedlings or by dividing older plants.

1

121

Medlar
Mespilus germanica

Rosaceae

Medlar was extensively cultivated in central Europe during the Middle Ages and currently its originally cultivated forms which have reverted to the wild can be found in the wine-growing regions. The medlar is native to Asia Minor and the Caucasus. It still grows wild in the Balkans, the Mediterranean, the Caucasus and Iran, and is cultivated in France, Italy, Spain and other warm regions, especially those where wine is produced. It grows well in damp, lime-rich, sun-warmed soils. Medlar is an undemanding species that withstands well even a polluted urban environment and is considerably resistant to frost. It regularly bears fruit as it is late flowering and therefore not damaged by frost. The fruits must be alowed to ripen fully. They are harvested after the first frosts and then left to soften, as then their pink or greenish pulp is tastier. Medlars have a slightly sweet to sourish taste, without any unpleasant bitterness. They are made into wines, syrups and marmalades in combination with plums or elderberries or are eaten raw. They are dietetically and medicinally valuable as they contain a considerable amount of tannins which can be used in the treatment of intestinal catarrh. They also contain 73 per cent water and 27 per cent dry matter, about 1 per cent proteins, 11—13 per cent sugars (mainly fructose and glucose), organic acids such as malic in amounts of about 1.15 per cent, pectins, cellulose, minerals, vitamin C, provitamin A and others.

Description
Medlar (1) is a very attractive shrub or tree. It has conspicuous flowers and its leaves turn yellow to red in the autumn. The tree itself reaches a height of up to 5 metres, wild forms having thorns on their branches, cultivars none. The leaves are spear-shaped and greyish felted on the underside and the flowers grow singly, opening in the second half of May. They are decorative, white and up to 5 cms in diameter. The outer casing of the flower has long tips which reach beyond the petals. The fruits (2) are small and globe- or pear-shaped, 1—3 cms across, and contain five hard seeds (3 — cross-section of the fruit). They are brown-green in colour, with a shorth stalk and a deep bowl-shaped casing with conspicuous tips.

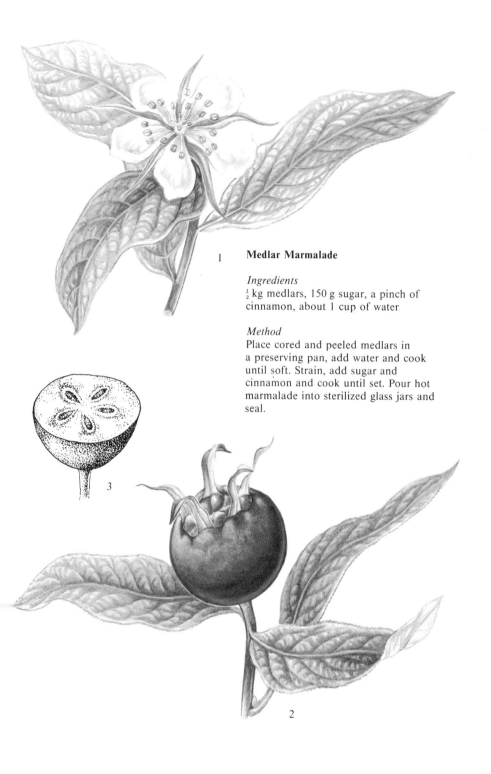

1 **Medlar Marmalade**

Ingredients
$\frac{1}{2}$ kg medlars, 150 g sugar, a pinch of cinnamon, about 1 cup of water

Method
Place cored and peeled medlars in a preserving pan, add water and cook until soft. Strain, add sugar and cinnamon and cook until set. Pour hot marmalade into sterilized glass jars and seal.

3

2

White Mulberry
Morus alba
Moraceae

White mulberry has been cultivated together with the black mulberry (*M. nigra*) since ancient times. It was particularly well known in China and Ancient Greece, where the fruits were believed to have great antidotal properties against poisons. The nations of Central Asia, in particular the ancient Tajiks, dried its fruits and ground them to a powder which was then added to desserts. Properly dried fruits last a long time and can be used instead of sugar. The leaves of white mulberry are the only food the caterpillars of the silkworm will eat. The white mulberry was imported to Europe from Asia. It now grows in southern Europe, the warmer areas of central Europe, in America, and may be cultivated in Britain. The fruits — that is the mulberries, ripen gradually from July to August. They have a sweet, somewhat insipid flavour, are about 1.5 cms long, and coloured white, pinkish or pale violet. They contain up to 22 per cent sugars, malic and citric acid, pectin, 5—20 mg vitamin C per 100 g of pulp, carotene, vitamin E, folic acid, vitamins B_1 and B_6, provitamin A and many mineral substances such as potassium and phosphorus. The fruit also contains up to 87 per cent water and can be used to prepare a tasty fruit drink. To every litre of juice put about $\frac{1}{4}$ litre water, 800 g sugar and juice of one lemon. It can also be made into a compote. Cider made from mulberries has a characteristic honey-like flavour. They also have mild curative properties aiding the workings of the intestine. The juice can be used in the treatment of sore throats and as an expectorant.

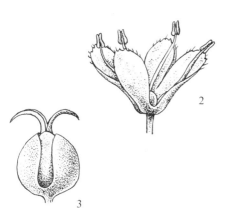

Description
White mulberry (1) is a tree with a grey trunk and brown branches. It has alternate, entire, round to oval leaves with short hair underneath. Some leaves have several asymmetrical lobes, others are complete. The flowers are unisexual with catkin-like floral arrangements. The male flowers (2) have free segments in their outer part and four stamens; the female flowers (3) have free and smooth segments and the superior ovary carries a smooth stigma. The fruits are mulberries — cylindrical, multiple fruits arising from the union of small dry seed pods on a fleshy covering — borne on long stalks. They ripen between July and

September, and when harvested they
easily drop off and release juice. In
Europe another three mulberry species
grow in the wild or are cultivated. These
are the black mulberry (*M. nigra*) with
dark red fruits, the red mulberry
(*M. rubra*) with bright red fruits and
M. trnaviensis which has the tastiest
fruits and which probably originated
from cross-breeding the black and red
mulberry.

1

Black Mulberry
Morus nigra
Moraceae

The black mulberry comes from Asia. Today it is cultivated for its fruits in the warmer regions of central Europe, in France, Italy, Spain and Britain. It grows best in wine-growing areas and is undemanding in its soil requirements. The leaves are less suitable than those of the white mulberry as food for the silkworm. Its fruits, which were once used as an aid to digestion, were also used to colour wine. The fruits and leaves may also be used medicinally. The dark red fruits which grow to a length of 2.5 cms are collected from July to September and are reminiscent of raspberries. When being collected they easily drop off and release their juice. They are more flavoursome than those of the white mulberry, are less sweet and contain more acids. They contain 14—16 per cent sugars, mainly glucose and fructose, about 1—1.6 per cent malic and citric acids, and up to 20 mg vitamin C per 100 g fresh fruit, carotene, B group vitamins, folic acid, vegetable colouring agents known as antocyanogens, pectins, minerals etc. In a mixture with other fruits they make a delicious compote, cider, syrup, marmalade or wine. They may also be eaten raw. They are effective in treating sore throats, coughs and constipation. Along with the fruit, the dried leaves of black mulberry can also be used. They contain a high percentage of calcium and other minerals, tannins and glucose and are helpful in diabetes by decreasing the sugar level in the blood. They can also be used to treat disorders of the pancreas and to prevent diarrhoea.

2

Description
Black mulberry (1) is a tree with a grey trunk and red-brown branches. Its alternate leaves are tough, broadly oval, usually with smooth edges and coarsely hairy on the underside. The flowers are unisexual. The male flowers have greenish free segments in the outer section and four stamens; the female flowers have free, hairy segments and the superior ovary carries a downy stigma. The flowers are pollinated by the wind. The mulberries (2) are in fact multiple fruits, reddish-purple in colour and composed of small, dry seed pods enclosed in a fleshy perianth.

Mulberry Syrup

Ingredients
1 litre mulberry juice, $\frac{1}{4}$ litre water, 800 g
sugar, juice of 2 lemons

1

Method
Boil sugar and water. Add juice, boil for
a short while, stir in lemon juice and
remove from heat. Pour the syrup into
bottles while warm and seal.

Common Marjoram, Oregano
Origanum vulgare   Labiatae

In folk medicine common marjoram has been employed since the earliest times. Hippocrates recommended it for strengthening the nerves and to cure lung diseases. In the Middle Ages it was in general use for speeding up the digestion, to treat constipation, ailing kidneys, female diseases, toothache, headache, sore throat, rheumatism and coughs. It is thus not surprising that it was considered to be a witches' herb. Some of its medicinal properties have been scientifically confirmed. Common marjoram grows in the temperate zone of Eurasia, reaching as far as the Himalayas and central Siberia. It was introduced to America and China and is cultivated in Spain, India, Italy, Greece and Mexico. The tops are collected in the wild when they begin to flower, that is between June and August, best before noon, when the volatile oil content is the highest. It should be dried in a shallow layer or suspended in bundles in the shade. Dry leaves and flowers are then rubbed off from the stems. They have a pleasant aroma and a bitterish spicy taste and serve both as a medicinal herb and a spice. The plant contains about 0.5 per cent volatile oil with thymol as its main component, also bitter principles, up to 8 per cent tannins, vitamin C and other elements. As a spice it has a similar taste and aroma to marjoram. Common marjoram is used to season forcemeats, sauces to accompany pasta, pizza and risotto. It is also used in herb mixtures with chilli and other aromatic herbs and goes well with lamb, fish, vegetable dishes, smoked and grilled meats, and cheese with basil, pepper and garlic. Marjoram is a spice used in Italian, French, Spanish and Mexican cuisines and has a calming influence on the digestive tract, improving both digestion and appetite.

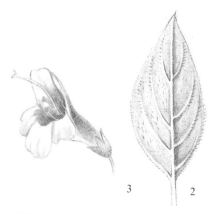

3   2

Description
Common marjoram (1) is a perennial warmth-loving plant. It grows on sunny slopes, in clearings, light woodland and in thickets. It thrives in areas ranging from lowlands to mountains but is more abundant in warm regions. It can be cultivated in a rockery. The woody root stem produces square, downy and usually reddish stems which reach a height of 60 cms. The opposite, short-stalked oval, hairy leaves (2) have

smooth or indistinctly toothed downy
edges. The lower leaves are the biggest
graduating to smaller leaves at the top.
The flowers (3) which grow in terminal
inflorescences have short stalks and
a bell-shaped five-toothed outer casing
and a two-lipped corolla which is
occasionally white but usually pinkish
red to carmine. They flower from July to
September. The fruits are nutlets (4). It
is a considerably variable species which
occurs in a number of different forms.

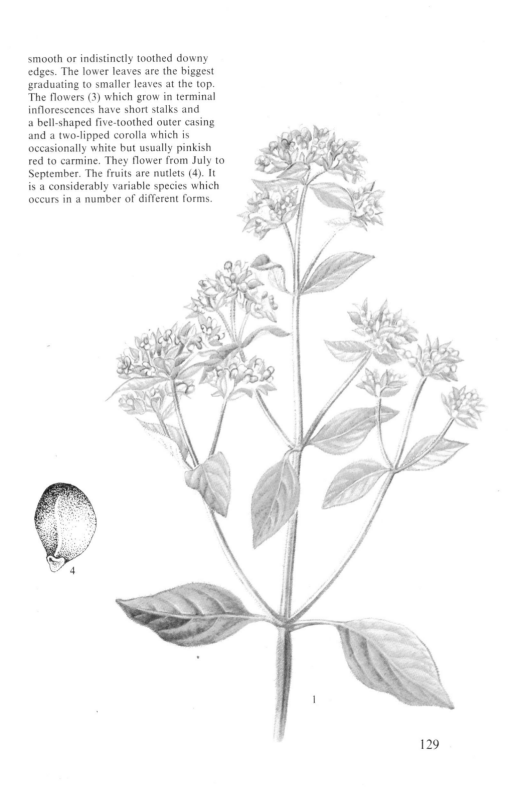

4

1

Wood-sorrel
Oxalis acetosella
Oxalidaceae

Wood-sorrel is widely distributed throughout Europe. It grows in the whole temperate zone of the northern hemisphere and in north Africa. It often forms continuous colonies in shady, damp forests, close to streams and sometimes in rotting wood. It may be present from lowlands up to the subalpine zone. The leaves, which are edible, are collected at the beginning of flowering, especially in spring or during the second flowering in the autumn. Wood-sorrel contains more than 2 per cent proteins, over 9 per cent saccharides and in terms of minerals a significant amount of calcium and magnesium, iron and phosphorus. In contains also about 80 mg vitamin C per 100 g, which is 2.5 times more than lemons, along with oxalic acid and its salts, mucilages, enzymes etc. The leaves are used to give a sour flavour to borshch or cream soups, sauces, mayonnaise, yoghurts, salads and drinks. It should not be used excessively since apart from beneficial elements it also contains the undesirable oxalic acid, which deprives the human body of calcium. Wood-sorrel is therefore used only in small quantities as a green spice. Wood-sorrel has a greater application in folk medicine. It has diuretic effects and it is recommended to chew its fresh leaves to treat inflamed gums and when crushed to dress wounds. In digestive disorders it is recommended to drink tea prepared from dried wood-sorrel. A drink made from the fresh leaves decreases fever. However, it is not often used as an officially recognized medicinal plant. It should·never be administered by amateurs, however, as it could have undesirable side-effects if used uncorrectly.

2

Description
Wood-sorrel (1) is a perennial, fragile plant reaching a height of 15 cms. It

130

spreads by its slender, creeping rootstock. It has no stem, and the rootstock produces stalked three-parted leaves (2) similar to clover. In cold or very hot weather the leaves become characteristically folded and bend over. The flowers (3), which appear in April and May, are whitish to pinkish with purple veins. In September to October they flower a second time when the flowers are smaller. The fruit (4) is a capsule which bursts when ripe and releases numerous seeds in its

neighbourhood. The autumn flowers, after fertilization, work their way into the ground where the fruits ripen. The plant has characteristic botanical features which make it unlikely to be confused with another species.
NOTE: Those who suffer from kidney stones and diseases of the urinary tract and from tuberculosis should avoid Wood-sorrel completely. Others should use it only in small quantities as a green spice, since it contains oxalic acid which is harmful.

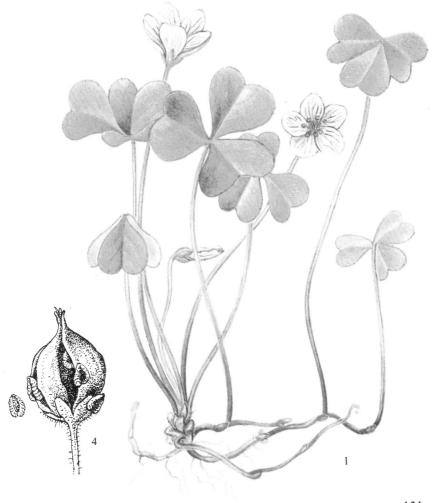

Greater Burnet-saxifrage
Pimpinella major

Umbelliferae

Greater burnet-saxifrage and burnet-saxifrage (*P. saxifraga*) can be easily confused with each other in the wild, but this is of no consequence as both species have similar uses. The plants have been known since ancient times. It was mainly the root of greater burnet-saxifrage which was widely used for medicinal purposes. The Romans employed it in the treatment of heart disease and male infertility, in the Middle Ages it was considered to be effective for the treatment of plague and cholera, and on a lighter level as a spice in beer. Greater burnet-saxifrage is an original European species and grows only in Europe today. It thrives in meadows in a moderately humid climate and in the proximity of forests from lowland altitudes to a height of 1.500 m above sea level, higher than burnet-saxifrage. Its young leaves which are bigger than those of the burnet-saxifrage are picked from the basal rosette before the stem is formed. The white to brown balsam-scented roots are dug up between March and May and in September. They are dried quickly in the shade and, because of the essential oil content, should be stored in dark containers with tightly fitting lids. The roots and tops of both species contain a golden-coloured essential oil made up of coumarins, tannins, resins, saponins, saccharides, vitamin C, carotene etc. The fresh young leaves of greater burnet-saxifrage may be finely chopped and added to soups, sauces, mayonnaise, spreads, stuffings and salads, and to season vegetables. Its leaves are not dried for use. The roots are only used in folk medicine, to treat coughs, hoarseness and inflammations of the upper respiratory tract. They also have mild diuretic effects.

Description
Greater burnet-saxifrage (1) is more robust than burnet-saxifrage (see next page) and reaches a height of one metre. Its spindle-shaped root resembles a small beet, being initially white in colour and turning brown with age. Its stem is prominently ridged, grooved, hollow, and covered with leaves up to the top. The leaves (2) have an odd number of leaflets, the topmost leaf usually having three lobes. The five-petalled, white or pink flowers (3) are arranged in a compound umbrella-shaped spray. The fruits are small dry double seed pods with five distinct ridges (4). The roots of

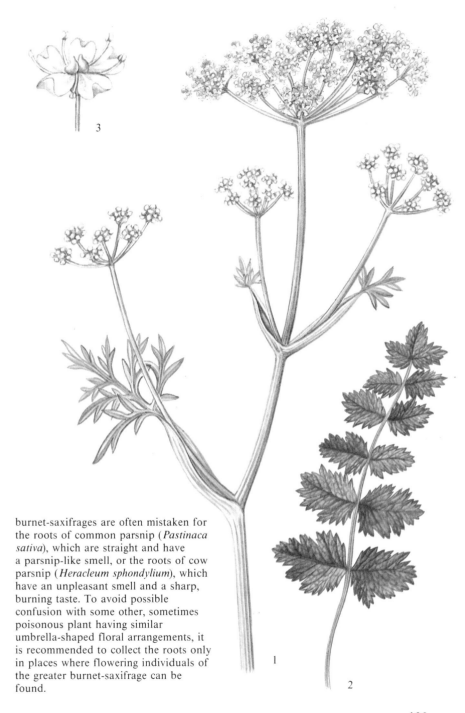

3

burnet-saxifrages are often mistaken for
the roots of common parsnip (*Pastinaca
sativa*), which are straight and have
a parsnip-like smell, or the roots of cow
parsnip (*Heracleum sphondylium*), which
have an unpleasant smell and a sharp,
burning taste. To avoid possible
confusion with some other, sometimes
poisonous plant having similar
umbrella-shaped floral arrangements, it
is recommended to collect the roots only
in places where flowering individuals of
the greater burnet-saxifrage can be
found.

1

2

Burnet-saxifrage
Pimpinella saxifraga
Umbelliferae

Burnet-saxifrage is native to all Europe, western Asia and Pakistan from where its presence extends into central Siberia. It also grows in North America and New Zealand, where it was introduced. Although it grows wild in dry grassy locations, such as slopes and meadows, it can be cultivated in the garden and in boxes. Burnet-saxifrage prefers a sunny location with a light or stony soil. The young leaves are collected by picking from the basal rosette early in spring between May and June before the stem is formed and before they become tough. The roots, which are nowadays only used medicinally, are collected in spring or autumn. They are used in the same way as the roots of greater burnet-saxifrage, for the treatment of diseases of the upper respiratory tract. Similarly, they were also used to spice beer. The leaves contain volatile oil, coumarins, saccharides, tannins, pectins, saponins, vitamin C, provitamin A, a large amount of calcium and potassium. They improve appetite, digestion and may be used to assist in the treatment of certain digestive disorders. They have a slightly sweet, hot, and mildly astringent taste with a hint of cucumber flavour. They are used cut up finely in soups, mayonnaise, herb butter, spreads, salads, in cream and yoghurt, for cold sauces, with grilled poultry, fish, vegetables etc. About 1 tbsp of cut leaves per person is usually used. Burnet-saxifrage is used in Italian, French, Spanish and also German and English cuisine, but should not be eaten in large quantities as it irritates the kidneys.

3

Description
Burnet-saxifrage (1) is a perennial, downy grey or smooth herb with a spindle-shaped root with its own characteristic smell and astringent taste. The leaves in the basal rosette are composed of an odd number of variously shaped leaflets (2). They are oval with toothed edges. The erect, branched, finely grooved stem reaching 20—50 cms in height develops later. The central stem leaves have a sheath and no

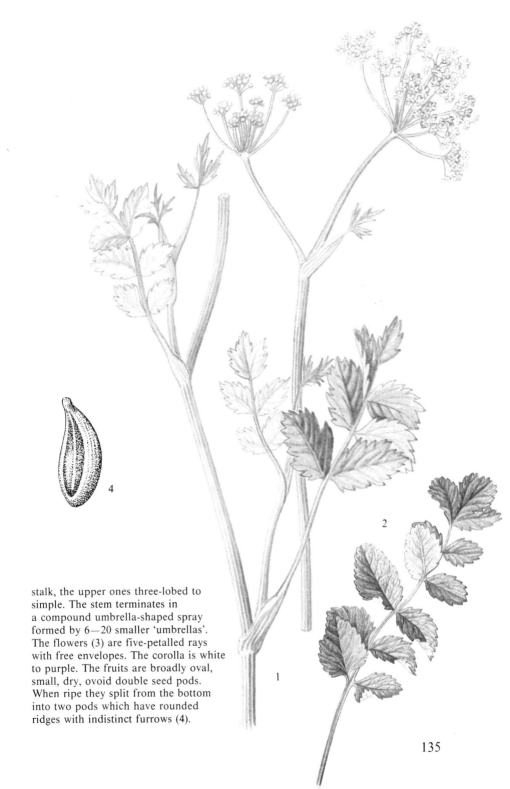

stalk, the upper ones three-lobed to
simple. The stem terminates in
a compound umbrella-shaped spray
formed by 6—20 smaller 'umbrellas'.
The flowers (3) are five-petalled rays
with free envelopes. The corolla is white
to purple. The fruits are broadly oval,
small, dry, ovoid double seed pods.
When ripe they split from the bottom
into two pods which have rounded
ridges with indistinct furrows (4).

135

Umbrella Pine
Pinus pinea

Pinaceae

Umbrella pine is a conifer with a characteristically umbrella-shaped crown. It is a warmth-loving tree from the Mediterranean, growing mostly in Italy, Greece, Yugoslavia, Portugal and Spain and also in North Africa and central Asia. It can be also found in some areas around the Black Sea and may be cultivated in Britain. The seeds of the umbrella pine are edible. They have a white kernel and their taste is similar to that of almonds, ripening in large broad cones in the third year. The large seeds of other pine species are also edible, for example those of *P. cembra* growing in the Tatra Mountains, *P. sibirica* growing in Siberia, the Urals and in the European part of the USSR, and the Korean pine (*P. koraiensis*). The seeds are eaten peeled, raw or roasted and often coated in sugar. They are used in the making of petit-fours and cakes and can also be added to meat and vegetable dishes. They contain 50—60 per cent fats, 5—6 per cent proteins, saccharides, vitamins B and C, minerals, resins etc. Oil pressed from the seeds is used in micro-technology, the production of paints, etc. The pine nuts also have medicinal properties — Avicenna recommended the kernels of umbrella pine as a healing, generally cleansing remedy. Folk medicine still uses an infusion made from pine nuts in treating gout, arthritis, diseases of the kidneys and of the bladder. The needles of the umbrella pine are a rich source of vitamin C (up to 250 mg per 100 g), carotene, and vitamin K. A vitamin-rich drink can be prepared from the young tips of small branches.

Description

The umbrella pine (1) is a deeply rooted tree reaching a height of up to 30 metres, with an erect, unbranched trunk. It forms a dense, at first spherical crown which later branches broadly outwards, extending up to 20 metres in diameter. The bark is greyish brown or reddish brown; when it is peeled off, an orange-red bark is revealed beneath. The wood is white, the needles (2) 10—15 cms long, tough and bright green. The cones are large, 10—15 cms long and 7—10 cms wide, glossy brown and sprinkled with resin. One usually contains up to one hundred seeds (3) covered by a very hard casing and with or without a wing. The umbrella pine is not cultivated in central Europe. It likes a warm climate and does not tolerate freezing temperatures.

136

2

1

3

137

Ribwort Plantain
Plantago lanceolata
Plantaginaceae

Ribwort plantain is one of the best known healing plants. It shares its habitats with the hoary plantain (*P. media*) and the great plantain (*P. major*). The two latter species are used only in folk medicine; in official therapy they are not recognized because of the low content of effective substances. Ribwort plantain grows all over Europe, in western Asia and North Africa, and was also introduced to a number of regions on all continents. It can be found in dry meadows, pastureland, lawns, fields, gardens and alongside roads from lowland regions to the mountains. The young leaves are the most suitable for culinary purposes and also for medicinal use. They are collected before the flowering stems develop, best in spring. It is possible to collect them even several times a year because the plants quickly regenerate. The leaves contain in particular mucilages, also antibiotics, the glycoside aucubin, tannins, flavonoids, bitter principles, proteins, enzymes, saponins, silicic acid, a large quantity of potassium and calcium and provitamin A. The fresh leaves contain over 70 mg vitamin C per 100 g. They are therefore a beneficial element for spring vegetable cuisine. In spring they may be added in small quantities to herb soups at a ratio of 1 tbsp per litre, to sauces or salads. They can even be coated in a savoury or sweet batter and fried. Plantain syrup is an excellent remedy for inflammation of the upper respiratory tract, coughs and also abdominal and intestinal disorders. It is in particular suitable for children. Plantain leaves can be dried for tea.

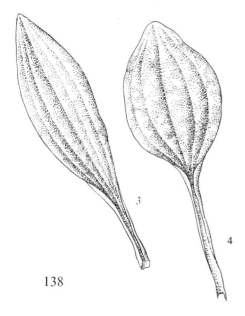

Description
Ribwort plantain (1) is a perennial herb with a short root and a rosette of basal leaves common in fields and gardens. Its leaves (2) are spear-shaped, erect and tapering at the base, with three to seven ribs on the blade. Scapes, bearing the terminal cylindrical brown spikes, grow from the middle of the rosette. Later the spike extends to reach a length of up to 4 cms. Four stamens with yellow anthers protrude on long filaments from the inconspicuous small flowers. The filaments are 2—3 times longer than the inner part of the flower. Ribwort plantain flowers from May to

September. Its fruit is a capsule and its
seeds become sticky in damp conditions.
Hoary plantain (*P. media*) has broadly
elliptic leaves which are pressed to the
ground; they have five to nine ribs and
their wedge-shaped base continues into
a short petiole (3). The prominent ribs
on the underside of the leaf are densely
hairy. Great plantain (*P. major*) has
larger, elliptic to almost oval shaped,
smooth leaves (4).

1

2

139

Water-pepper
Polygonum hydropiper

Polygonaceae

Water-pepper is one of the oldest medicinal plants. Long ago its seed pods were used as substitute for real pepper. Mention is made of it by Dioscorides, who himself used the name 'water-pepper' and so distinguished it from black and white pepper. Water-pepper grows in the temperate zone of Eurasia, in North Africa and North America. The tops are collected at the beginning of flowering and may be used both fresh and dried. They have a peppery taste which is due to substances present in the glands of the leaves and the stem. Water-pepper contains up to 4 per cent tannins, bitter principles, flavonoids, mucilages, a sharply tasting volatile oil, rutin, glucoside and organic acids. It contains as much as 140 mg vitamin C per 100 g of green tops. It also contains vitamins H and K and traces of vitamin D and E, and is an excellent source of minerals, such as iron, calcium, phosphorus and magnesium. The tops are used fresh, 1—2 tsp of leaves per person, in salads, spreads, soups, sauces, forcemeats and stuffings, but large amounts should not be eaten. Dried tops are used in the preparation of tea to lessen the bleeding of haemorrhoids and menstruation or to bathe wounds and rinse the mouth. They have excellent styptic and slight diuretic properties.

Lamb Ragout

Ingredients
1 kg lamb shoulder, 2 onions, 150 g root vegetables, 2—3 tbsp butter, 1 tbsp plain flour, 5 tbsp finely cut sorrel leaves, 1 cup cream, $1\frac{1}{2}$ cups stock, 1 egg yolk, 1 tsp finely chopped water-pepper tops, salt

Method
Cut meat into cubes. Clean and coarsely grate vegetables, chop onion and fry a little in butter; add meat, water-pepper and salt and fry briefly. Add flour and stir, pour in 1 cup of stock and braise. Add remaining stock as necessary. When the meat is tender, add sorrel, cook a little, add cream with beaten yolk and set aside straight away. Serve with pasta, dumplings or rice.

Description
Water-pepper (1) is an annual, glabrous, up to 50 cm tall herb. It grows abundantly in permanently wet soils, in damp meadows, close to the sources of water, on damp tips etc. from low-lying to submountainous regions. It grows well in damp, nitrogen-rich but lime-free soils. It forms an articulated stem with swollen nodes. The leaves (2) are alternate, short-stalked, and spear-shaped, with transparent dots

1

which are in fact submersed essential oil glands. The flowers are small with a greenish pink hue and are arranged in terminal sparse false spikes. The fruit is small and dry.

141

Purslane
Portulaca oleracea   Portulacaceae

Purslane probably comes from Asia Minor, where it grows in the wild up to a height of five thousand metres above sea level. At present it is widespread throughout the warmer areas of all European countries and in North and South America. It thrives everywhere if it has enough light and warmth. Wild purslane was subject to wide cultivation, which led to the origin of both cultivated vegetable forms and decorative varieties with large, coloured flowers. Purslane has been used as a vegetable, spice and medicinal plant since the time of the ancient Egyptians. It was also very popular in England in the Middle Ages. The useful parts of the plant are the young fleshy stems with leaves. They are harvested from late spring and during the summer, but only until the plant begins to flower as later they become coarse and have a sharp taste. The young parts have a pleasant, slightly sour and somewhat salty and spicy flavour. They are rich in carotene, vitamins B_1, B_2 and vitamin C. They also contain a considerable amount of mineral substances. They are effective in treating stomach acidity, heartburn, flatulence and other diseases. Purslane also has diuretic effects and an overall calming influence. During cooking it loses its aroma and is therefore added fresh, finely chopped, to finished meals. It can be prepared in a salad with vinegar, oil, salt and pepper or may be added to lettuce, cucumber and tomato salads. Its leaves and young shoots are added to vegetable soups and sauces just before serving, to mayonnaise, herb butters and spreads. The leaves can be pickled in vinegar as a substitute for capers.

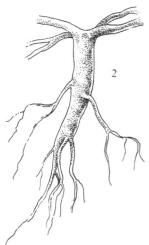

2

3

Description

Purslane (1) is an annual herb with a spherical, shallow root (2) and with creeping or semi-erect, forked, up to 30 cm long stems. It grows alongside roads and in the gaps between paving stones, alongside houses, fences, on banks, in gardens, orchards and vineyards and vegetable plots. In fertile soils with sufficient moisture it forms dense flat tufts up to one metre in diameter. It also grows during periods of serious water shortage when other weeds dry up. However, it is sensitive to a drop in temperature, particularly at temperatures below freezing point. The stem and the leaves are fleshy. The leaves are small, elongated, with very short stalks. The flowers are white, yellowish to red with distinct bracts. The fruit is a capsule containing tiny, kidney-shaped, brown-black seeds with a small blunt projection (3). The seeds germinate quickly so that purslane is a weed which is rather difficult to eradicate, especially in warm wine-growing regions.

1

Wild Cherry
Prunus avium
Rosaceae

Wild cherry stones have been found in pile dwellings of Neolithic man. The original home of the wild cherry was the Near East, the deciduous forests of the Caucasus, Crimea, Ukraine, Moldavia and the Balkans. Its distribution is carried out mostly by birds. The cultivated varieties are known from the 4th century B. C. It is possible to find many types of wild cherry, its various forms and hybrids of wild and cultivated varieties with small fruit. The well ripened fruits are collected in the wild from June to July. They are a source of valuable nutritive substances and are particularly suitable for children. They contain about 10—15 per cent sugars in an easily digested form, about 10 per cent pectins, 2 per cent organic acids, namely malic and citric, a large amount of provitamin A, about 10 mg vitamin C per 100 g fresh fruit, vitamins of the B group, folic and nicotinic acid. Furthermore there are anthocyanic pigments as well as mineral substances such as calcium, phosphorus, iron, magnesium, potassium and other elements. Cherries promote blood, bone and teeth formation; they improve the functioning of the kidneys and liver and increase blood circulation. They are beneficial against rheumatism and the cherry juice lowers fever. The fresh fruits should not be eaten in large quantities and water should not be drunk immediately afterwards, as cherries have a propensity to swell significantly and this could happen even in the digestive tract. They are used in the production of ciders, wines, brandies, jams combined with red currants, compotes with gooseberries, and can also be used in desserts. When dried, they can be used instead of raisins. The fruit stalks have medicinal properties: they are dried and the infusion made from them can be used to treat diarrhoea, coughs and common colds.

Description
The wild cherry (1) is a low-growing tree with an ovoid crown and smooth, greyish brown bark. It grows on slopes, at the edges of forests, especially in deciduous and mixed woods with oaks, hornbeams, limes, ashes etc. It thrives in lowland regions as well as submountainous areas and is undemanding in terms of soil. Its various cultivated forms are grown as fruit trees and a double-flowered variety as an ornamental. The leaves are

144

alternate, dull, long and oval, pointed at the tip, with serrated edges. They have two red glands on the leaf stalk underneath the blade. The flowers develop in umbrella-shaped sprays on short stalks 3—6 cms long in the second half of May. They are white and have many stamens with yellow anthers. The stoned fruits ripen in the middle of June, most often in July. They are light to dark red, smooth and juicy.

1

145

Cherry Plum
Prunus cerasifera

Rosaceae

The cherry plum is an adaptable species that crossbreeds in the wild with sloe and bullace. It is commonly used as a stock for grafting cultivated forms of Bullace, especially in dry regions. It is also planted as an ornamental tree, particularly the ssp. *pissartii* with its dark red leaves and large red fruits, which are also edible. Escapes from cultivation with variously shaped leaves and fruits can often be found in the wild. Similarly spontaneous crossbreeds with sloe can be found, with fruits larger than those of sloe. The original wild form of cherry plum grows in the Caucasus, Central Asia, Iran, Asia Minor and also in the Balkans, where it forms large colonies at high altitudes. A related species, *P. caspica,* also grows in the Caucasus. The well ripened fruits of cherry plum are harvested by shaking the tree. Their taste varies; some are sweeter, others slightly bitter and sour. They contain up to 10 per cent sugar — mainly fructose and glucose, malic and citric acids, tannins, minerals, and large amounts of pectin etc. 100 g pulp contains about 16 mg of vitamin C and up to 8 mg provitamin A. The fruits may be dried or made into marmalade or wine. In Georgia and Armenia they are made into a sharp sauce to accompany grilled meats. In folk medicine in Asia an infusion from the fruit is recommended to treat coughs and inflammations of the upper respiratory tract.

Description

Cherry plum (1) is a shrub or tree with slender branches reaching a height of between four and fifteen metres. The leaves have a variable shape — they can be oval to spear-shaped and between 2 and 10 cms long and 2 and 4 cms wide. The flowers develop singly or in twos; they are white and pink, appearing early in spring from March to April, earlier than the cultivated bullace. The fruits are smaller, oval or spherical, yellow or brownish-red (2) and contain a stone which usually adheres to the flesh (3 — longitudinal section).

Cherry Plum Chutney

Ingredients
$1\frac{1}{2}$ kg Cherry plums, 1 glass of vinegar, 1 tsp salt, 300 g sugar, 2 cloves of garlic, $\frac{1}{2}$ tsp ground ginger, a pinch of ground cloves, cinnamon, pepper and chilli powder, $\frac{1}{2}$ tsp grated lemon rind

2

Method
Cover fruit with water, boil until soft,
strain, add vinegar, salt, crushed garlic
and spice and, stirring continuously,
allow to thicken. Pour hot chutney into
small sterilized glass containers, allow to
cool, then seal. Use with roast and
grilled meat.

1

3

147

Sour Cherry, Dwarf Cherry
Prunus cerasus
Rosaceae

Sour cherry comes from western Asia. It grows in the wild both at low and high altitudes. It was introduced into cultivation later than the sweet cherry; however, it was known as early as the Middle Ages. Wild forms are not known and cultivars probably developed by crossing the wild cherry with *P. fruticosus,* which still grows wild in the forest-steppe area of the Caucasus and Asia Minor. In Europe sour cherries escaped from cultivation grow freely on dry slopes in shrub or tree forms. They are less demanding in terms of soil than the sweet cherry. The shrub form can be found particularly at higher altitudes, where it spreads by its suckers to form continuous growths. The stalks and leaves are all collected for use. The fruits can be used in the same way as those of the cultivated varieties. They contain up to 2 per cent organic acids — malic, citric, succinic, salicylic etc., 13—20 mg vitamin C per 100 g fresh fruits, a smaller quantity of provitamin A, vitamins of the B group, about 8 per cent sugars (mainly glucose), up to 2 per cent pectins, a considerable amount of salts of potassium, calcium, phosphorus and iron, antocyanic colouring substances, tannins and other elements. They contain approximately 8 per cent water. Juice from the fruits helps remove unwanted metabolic products from the body and decreases fever to some extent. It is recommended in cases of anaemia, liver disorders and digestive troubles. The fruits are used to make juices, syrups, alcoholic and soft drinks, jams, compotes, soups, desserts and confectionery, often in combination with other less flavourful fruits. They can be also dried. The leaves are used when pickling sauerkraut and gherkins and the fruit stalks are used as one of the components of teas used in slimming diets and for urinary and kidney complaints.

Description
Sour cherry (1) is a small tree or shrub with slender, flexible branches which along with the trunk have a smooth bark. The leaves are alternate, stalked, broadly elliptic with pointed tips and serrated edges. The stalked flowers (2) appear when the leaves bud; in the wild forms this often occurs for the second time at the end of summer. The

five-petalled flowers (3 — longitudinal section) have white petals, a large number of stamens and a superior ovary. Sour cherry flowers later than sweet cherry and is therefore less threatened by late frosts. The fruit is a globe-shaped, red and stoned drupe with soft flesh, ripening in July and August. It has a distinct sweet and sour flavour.

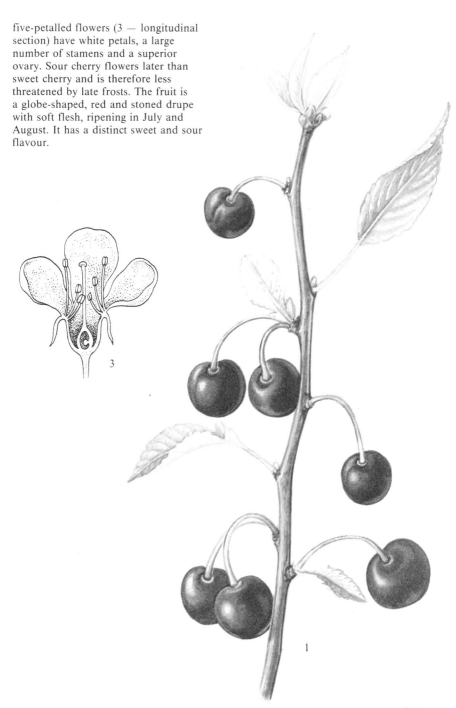

149

Bullace
Prunus insititia

Rosaceae

One of the ancestors of the bullace is probably sloe. Currently in existence are varieties with variously coloured fruits, ranging from white, green, yellow, pink and purple to dark blue and violet. Wild forms of bullace grow in the Caucasus; individual trees that have reverted to the wild, however, can also be found in central Europe. They have small, round to oval fruits, which are blue-black in colour. Their flesh is softer and has a finer flavour than that of sloes. Nevertheless it is so astringent that the fruit is usually left on the trees until November and is only collected after the first frosts. Bullaces contain 4—9 per cent sugars — mainly glucose and fructose — also about 1 per cent organic acids, namely malic and citric, and traces of salicylic and oxalic acids. The water content is about 80 per cent and their content of mineral substances exceeds that of apples and pears. They have a high content of potassium and phosphorus, but less magnesium, iron and calcium. The fruits also contain carotene, tannins, vitamin B_1 and B_2 and 5—20 mg of vitamin C per 100 g pulp. The fruits of all types of bullace are diuretic and are recommended for their high content of potassium in the treatment of rheumatism, gout, liver and kidney diseases and for diseases associated with blood circulation. They are eaten fresh or made into compotes, marmalades, wine, fruit sauces etc. They are added to desserts, savoury and meat dishes.

Description

Bullace (1) is a shrub or a tree. It is less thorny but larger than sloe. The leaves are elliptical with serrated edges, smooth and dull above, finely downy pubescent beneath. The five-petalled flowers (2) grow singly on hairy stalks. They are pure white or yellowish in colour. The fruits are dark blue with a compressed stone to which the flesh adheres (3 — longitudinal section).

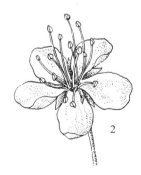

2

Tkemali Sauce

Ingredients

1 kg bullaces, 1 cup of water, 1 small head of garlic, 2 tbsp chopped dill, 3 tbsp ground coriander, 2 tsp sweet paprika, 2 tbsp chopped fresh mint, a pinch of hot paprika, salt

Method

Add water to bullaces and boil until soft. Then strain and heat paste, adding water if necessary to reach a consistency of sour cream. Add crushed garlic, herbs and salt and cook for a short while. Serve cold with grilled meat.

1

3

151

Sloe, Blackthorn
Prunus spinosa   Rosaceae

The fact that man collected the fruits of sloe as early as neolithic times is confirmed by the finds of seeds in neolithic pile dwellings. Ancient physicians used the thickened juice from the fruits to treat intestinal catarrhs. The fruits and flowers have long proved useful in folk medicine. Sloe grows throughout Europe reaching as far as southern Scandinavia, North Africa and Iran in Asia. It is noted for its great variability; in the wild it crossbreeds easily, for example with cherry plum. The fruits are collected when fully ripe or even overripe. They contain a lot of tannins, sugars, about 20 mg vitamin C per 100 g pulp, provitamin A, vitamins of the B group, organic acids and glycoside amygdaline, which is poisonous in large quantities but tolerable in small doses. Mineral substances are represented mainly by calcium, potassium and magnesium. Sloes are effective against diarrhoea, stomach disorders and diseases of urinary tract. They are very astringent and can be eaten fresh in small quantities only, and best of all, after the first frosts. They are most suitable for compotes made from bland-tasting fruits, for wine making, liqueurs and syrups. They are preserved with sugar in wine and served with game or can be preserved in honey to make a compote. They can be also dried for tea. The flowers also have medicinal properties, containing about 0.4 per cent flavonoid glycosides, also traces of hydrocyanic acid, sugar and tannins. Tea made from the flowers in a ratio of 2 tsp flowers per 1 cup, in contrast to that of the fruits, has mild laxative effects; it also speeds up the metabolism, has anti-inflammatory effects and is also recommended in the treatment of the common cold.

NOTE: Care should be taken when using sloes. They should only be eaten in small amounts (not by children) and should never be used medicinally by amateurs.

2

152

Description

Sloe (1) is a thorny, densely branched shrub. It often grows in groups or in vast colonies, spreading by its rootstocks and reaching a height of up to 3 metres. It tolerates well both dry and warm conditions and lime in the soil and is quite undemanding in its nutritional requirements. It grows on sunny slopes, pastureland, alongside roads, in gorges, on banks and in fallow fields. Early in spring its young downy shoots produce spherical flower and leaf buds. It flowers early, from March to April, before the leaves appear. The flowers, mostly arranged in groups, are white and five-petalled, with a large number of stamens. The leaves are oval, hairy beneath, and have serrated edges. The fruits (2) are small-stoned, globe-shaped and blue-black with a frosted appearance characteristic of plums.

1

Lungwort, Jerusalem Cowslip
Pulmonaria officinalis   Boraginaceae

Early in spring the lungwort's fine flowers open in sparse deciduous woods and groves close to water. The flowerbuds are pink and as they open out gradually turn purple and blue. The reason for the colour change in the flowers is the vegetable pigment, antocyanogen, which changes colour according to the acidity of its cellular juice. This is not an isolated phenomenon in nature. Lungwort grows throughout the temperate zone of Europe from Great Britain to the Urals, being particularly abundant in central Europe. Its young leaves are collected from March to May, and contain up to 4 per cent silicic acid, up to 10 per cent tannins, 9 per cent saponins, flavonoids, resins, mucilage, and up to 50 mg vitamin C per 100 g as well as calcium, potassium and phosphorus, with trace elements and other substances. Its leaves are used in the preparation of spring salads, particularly in England. They can also be added to herb soups, soft cheese spreads, stuffings and forcemeats and have a slightly 'gluey' flavour. Lungwort belongs to one of the oldest known medicinal plants. Because of its leaves' resemblance to diseased lungs, medieval medical practice, which worked to a larger extent by association, recommended the use of a tea made from it and sweetened with honey to treat lung diseases.

4

Description
Lungwort (1) is a perennial herb which reaches a height of 30 cms. The slender cylindrical root stem (2) produces erect, sparsely branched flower-bearing stems. The entire plant is covered with sparse, rough hairs. The basal leaves (3) have long stalks with a broad oval to spear-shaped blade which has whitish spots although sometimes these are missing. The five-petalled flowers (4) have short stalks. The calyx is bell-shaped, with five teeth, and the corolla is purple, deepening in shade at a later stage. Another lungwort, *P. obscura,* with dark green unspotted leaves and shorter leaf stalks is also collected for culinary and medicinal purposes.

Beef Soup with Herbs

Ingredients
200 g beef, 1 carrot, 1 onion, 3 cloves of
garlic or several leaves of wild garlic,
3 tbsp barley, 2 cups of mixed
herbs—daisy, lungwort and goutweed—,
salt and wild or garden chives.

Method
Add $1\frac{1}{2}$ litres water and salt to meat and
boil until ulmost tender. Add chopped
carrot, onion and rinsed barley and boil
until soft. Then add finely chopped
herbs and crushed garlic and cook for
a further 5—10 minutes.

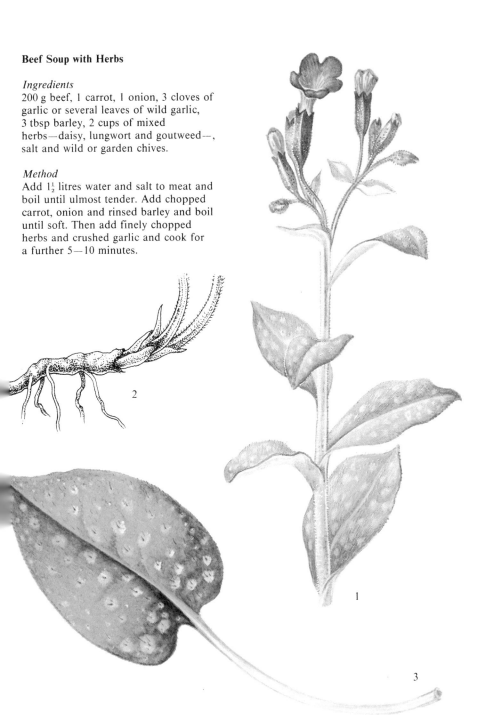

2

1

3

Pear
Pyrus
Rosaceae

About sixty pear species grow in the temperate and subtropical zones of the northern hemisphere, having originated in Greece. There are about 1,500 cultivated varieties, but only a few dozen of any real worth. The main areas inhabited by wild pear species are the Far East, the Caucasus and around the Mediterranean Sea. The species most frequently encountered is *P. communis,* which can also be found growing wild in central and western Europe, Transcaucasia, Asia Minor, Northern Iran and the Balkans. Pears growing in the wild vary in quality. Their fruits take many different shapes and are not as suitable to use fresh than those of the cultivated varieties. They can, however, be processed into ciders, vinegar and wine, or dried and minced for use as a dessert topping. They used to be pickled in vinegar and spice in the same way as gherkins. These pears can be added to marmalades and ciders made from bland-tasting fruits to intensify their flavour. Pears contain about 80 per cent water, are low in calories and therefore suitable for slimming diets. They have about 5—13 per cent fruit sugars, about 1 per cent pectin, 3 per cent cellulose and 0.2 per cent organic acids. In terms of minerals they contain a large percentage of potassium and therefore have diuretic effects. As they contain small amounts of sodium and chlorine, they are recommended for salt-free diets. Furthermore they contain tannins (about 5—20 mg vitamin C per 100 g), provitamin A, vitamins B_1 and B_2 and a number of other active elements. The tannins and pectin present in pears protect the mucous membrane of the stomach and intestines. The fresh or cooked fruit or the juice are also recommended for blood circulation problems and for kidney complaints. Pears are effective in the treatment of constipation and partially reduce fever.

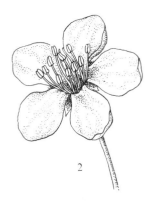

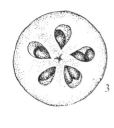

Description
Wild pears (1) usually grow in the form
of a tree. They are less resistant to frost
and less prone to attack by insects than
apple trees but bear more fruit. Their
five-petalled flowers (2) are white or
pink with a large number of stamens.
They bear variously shaped fleshy fruit
with a core, usually green or yellow.
Around the core (3—cross section of the
fruit) are scleroids, which are hard
scales formed by stone cells. In some
cultivars or seeded trees these may be
absent.

1

157

Black Currant
Ribes nigrum

Saxifragaceae

Black currant still grows wild in northern and central Europe and to the east as far as Manchuria. It can be found in deciduous and mixed forests in damp to wet soils from lowlands up to a thousand metres above sea level. Cultivated varieties of black currant originated through the domestication of wild species. It was first cultivated for its fruit at the end of the 17th century in France, then in England and later all over Europe. The fruits of black currant are very high in vitamins and other nutritional substances, therefore having a beneficial effect on the metabolism. They also have a diuretic effect. The vitamin C content of black currants is 4 per cent, 5—10 times more than that of lemons. Also contained in the fruit is provitamin A in larger quantities than oranges, many vitamins of the B group, so-called vitamin P (rutin), bioflavonoids, a large amount of pectin, cellulose, antocyanic pigments, tannins and a volatile oil. Furthermore they contain about 4 per cent organic acids with bactericidal properties, 8—16 per cent saccharides, mainly fruit sugars, potassium, iron, calcium and magnesium. The calorific value of the fruits is relatively low, so is useful for those of us who are watching our weight. The juice improves the elasticity of veins and is therefore recommended in pregnancy or during convalescence. An infusion made from dried fruits or juice mixed with honey is effective in the treatment of the common cold, mouth inflammations and sore throat. The fruits have a rather unpleasant smell which lessens a little when they are processed. The vitamin C is present in a fairly resistant form so that a relatively high percentage may be preserved in carefully prepared compotes and juices. The fruits may be used to make jams, jellies, juices, marmalades, compotes and liqueurs. They are suitable for desserts, soups and sauces, and the fresh leaves are used when spicing pickled gherkins and sauerkraut.

Description
Black currant (1) is a shrub which reaches a height of two metres with branches which are green at first, later turning a reddish brown. The stalked leaves are alternate, 3—5 lobed, with numerous glands on the underside which contain a volatile oil. The drooping sprays of bell-shaped,

158

1

yellow-green to red five-petalled flowers
(2) appear from April to May. The fruits
are long-stalked, spherical, black berries
dotted with glands and containing seeds
in juicy flesh; the whole plant has
a characteristic smell. Black currant
occurs in a large number of varieties
and is important in the production of
honey.

Dog Rose
Rosa canina
Rosaceae

Dog rose is the most widespread wild rose in Europe. It is a greatly variable species; it has about 13 small species with numerous cross-breeds. Its hips have a vitamin C content of 100—1000 mg per 100 g pulp, also present are provitamin A, vitamins of the B group, vitamin P and K and vitamin E (mainly in the achenes). Vitamin C remains in the hips even after cooking. They also contain up to 3 per cent tannins, inverted sugar, sucrose, about 10 per cent pectin, citric and malic acids, volatile oil, mucilages and flavonoid glycosides. They also contain phosphorus, calcium, potassium, iron and magnesium. Hips have considerable medicinal properties as well. They are not only effective against spring fatigue and hypovitaminosis, but increase resistance to diseases such as the common cold and influenza, and are useful in convalescence, as well as encouraging digestion and the formation of blood and also have a diuretic effect. The fruits should be collected when fully ripe and firm but not overripe. They can be made into preserves, wines, ketchups, soups and sauces for game. They are used commercially in the production of juices and syrups. When prepared at home, the hips should be destalked and the internal hairs removed by washing. They can be dried to make a tea which should be taken cold as a refreshing drink in cases of fever. Hips of all the rose species are edible, only the fruits of hybrid roses with large and numerous flowers are not suitable. Rose petals can be also used in the kitchen in the preparation of honey, syrups and preserves.

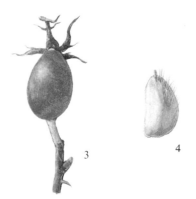

3

4

Description
Dog rose (1) is a shrub with long, arching, thorny branches, the flower-bearing stems having no thorns. It is not demanding, growing on slopes, alongside roads, on banks, in thickets, on rocky slopes, and along edges of woods up to a height of one thousand metres above sea level. As its numbers are gradually decreasing in the wild, rose growers have now begun to improve various wild rose species in order to produce large-fruited varieties. The leaves (2) are alternate, consisting of 5—7 serrated leaflets. The flowers,

which open from May to June, are
five-petalled, with a large number of
stamens and with pink or sometimes
white central petals. They grow on stalks
which are up to 2 cms in length. The
ripe hip (3) is bright red and contains
small yellow downy seed pods (4). It
retains a remnant of the calyx on top.

161

Japanese Rose
Rosa rugosa
Rosaceae

Native to northern China, Korea and Japan, this rose is often cultivated for decorative purposes in gardens and parks. It can also be
found, having reverted to its wild form, in the open countryside in
Britain. It is frost resistant, and even grows and bears fruit at 600 metres above sea level. The fruits are collected at the end of August and
in September, when fully ripe, firm and not frozen. The petals, collected throughout the summer, can also be used in the kitchen. Hips
from Japanese rose contain over 23 per cent dry matter, about 900 mg
vitamin C per 100 g flesh, over 13 per cent sugars and up to 14 mg of
carotene in 100 g dry pulp. They also contain mineral substances,
pectin, organic acids, flavonoid glycosides, vitamins of the B group,
vitamins P and K, tannins etc. Hips are well suited for processing due
to their large pulp content. Because of their vitamin C content, which
is very resistant and remains in considerable quantities even after processing, hips are an extremely valuable source of that vitamin. The
drying process begins at a high temperature, which destroys enzymes
responsible for breaking down vitamin C, after which drying is completed in a warm, airy place. It must be done quickly, otherwise the
hips easily become mouldy. Dried hips are used to make a tea which
has diuretic effects, improves vision and skin condition and generally
stimulates resistance to disease. Fresh hips may be used to make preserves, pastes, jellies and petit fours, and can also be candied. Juice
pressed from them can be made into syrup or wine. The dried petals
of the flower may be used to make tea, fresh ones for wines, syrups or
jam. They can also be preserved in honey.

2

Description
Japanese rose (1) is a shrub reaching
a height of up to three metres. The
leaves have indistinct ribs, are glossy,
wrinkled, dark green, and greyish
underneath. The branches are densely
covered with slender thorns. The
flowering season is quite long, the shrub
often flowering whilst some of the fruits
are ripening. The flowers occur in

clusters of 3—6, between 6 and 10 cms
in diameter, and are coloured carmine
purple, dark pink or white. The fruits
(2—longitudinal section) are spherical,
rather shrivelled, smooth, brick red hips.
They are very fleshy, the pulp forming
up to 80 per cent, seeds 20 per cent of
the plant matter. They are considerably
large, the diameter of the hip sometimes
reaching as much as 2.5 cms.

Soft-leaved Rose
Rosa villosa   Rosaceae

The soft-leaved rose grows wild in Europe and western Asia. Along with *R. rugosa, R. cinnamomea* and other roses, it is intensively cultivated to produce large-fruited varieties which sometimes revert to the wild. The fruits ripen at the end of August, and are collected when firm and ripe. Later they become soft and often split, especially in rainy weather. They should be picked in dry weather in order to preserve their greatest possible vitamin C content. When processed by heat, the fruits are sterilized for twenty minutes at the most and when cleaning them it is important just to cut them and not to crush them. The drying process is begun at a temperature of $80-100\,°C$, which is later lowered to $35-40\,°C$. The hips have about 26 per cent dry matter, over 1,500 mg vitamin C per 100 g pulp, about $13-14$ per cent sugars and other valuable substances. They are a rich source of carotenoids and provide pigments valuable for health, e. g. carotenes, lycopene, xanthophyll. They also contain pectins, mucilages, vitamins K, P and E as well as iron, potassium, phosphorus, calcium and magnesium. They have similar medicinal effects to those of other rose hip species. In the kitchen they may be used to make ketchups, marmalades, pastes, soups, sauces to accompany game, and for juices and syrups. The cleaned hips are sometimes preserved in honey. The flowers can be used to make wine and syrup, and just like other types of wild rose the young shoots and leaves may also be eaten as a salad in combination with other vegetables.

Rose Hip Sauce

Description
Soft-leaved rose (1) is a densely branching shrub reaching a height of up to two metres. The leaves consist of 5—7 grey-green leaflets with a felted underside. The flowers (2), which grow either singly or in groups of 2—3, are pink and not very elaborate, measuring only 3—5 cms in diameter. The hips are bright red, glossy, sparsely hairy, with a large outer casing of leaves. They are spherical to broadly egg-shaped or pear-shaped, (3 — longitudinal section), with a high pulp content.

Ingredients
$\frac{1}{2}$—1 kg hips, $\frac{1}{8}$ litre cream, $\frac{1}{8}$ litre white wine, 1 clove, 1 tsp icing sugar, 3 tbsp hip paste, 2 tbsp tomato paste, 1 tsp lemon juice, ground pepper, salt

Method
Clean hips removing calyx and seeds, add water, boil until soft and strain. Boil wine with sugar and clove. Add hip and tomato paste and strained hips, lemon juice, pour in cream, add salt and pepper and bring to the boil. Remove sauce from heat and serve with game.

1

2

3

165

Blackberry, Bramble
Rubus fruticosus Rosaceae

The genus *Rubus* is considerably varied and present in almost all parts of the world. As well as occurring as a wild shrub, it is also cultivated. The largest number of its species grows in North America, but it is also possible to find many species and subspecies in Europe. *R. fruticosus* occurs most frequently and forms dozens of different subspecies and crossbreeds. There are no special points to take into account when collecting blackberries since the fruits of all species growing in Europe are edible. They contain up to 14 per cent sugars, 0.5—1.5 per cent mainly malic and citric acids, mucilages, pectins, anthocyanic glycosides, about 35 mg vitamin C per 100 g pulp, provitamin A, and vitamins from the B group. In terms of minerals they contain compounds of potassium, magnesium, calcium, iron, copper and magnanese. Blackberries are most nutritious when eaten fresh. Their juice has mild calming effects and is recommended for neuroses resulting from crisis. They can be made into juices, jams, soups, compotes, syrups, wines and liqueurs, and are added to desserts. The leaves also have medicinal properties, being bactericidal, antidiarrhoeal and diuretic. They stimulate the metabolism and are therefore recommended for metabolic disorders. They contain 5—14 per cent tannins, flavonoid glycosides, pectins, mineral salts, 90 mg of vitamin C per 100 g, provitamin A etc. The dried and also fermented leaves are used in tea mixtures, for example with raspberry leaves and the tops of sweet woodruff.

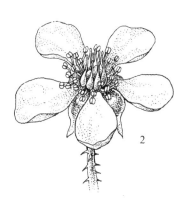

Description
Blackberry (1) is a shrub with thorny, creeping, woody shoots. It grows in thickets, along the edges of woods, in clearings, along fences and roads, on banks and in coastal thickets. Its prickly stems arch towards the ground, sometimes its tips root and in this way often form impenetrable thickets. Stems of two years and older bear flowers; the annual shoots are infertile. The leaves are alternate, prickly, and composed of three to five oval, pointed leaflets with serrated toothed edges. They have soft short hairs on top and are white-felted underneath. The flowering period lasts from May to July. The five-petalled

flowers (2), white or pink with a large
number of stamens and pistils, are
arranged in loose sprays. The ripe fruits
(3) are collected from August to
September. The blackberry (4) consists
of a cluster of tiny black, carmine red or
blue frosted spheres. In contrast to
raspberry, the compound fruit of which
separates from the receptacle when ripe,
blackberries are collected with their
receptacle still attached.

Raspberry
Rubus idaeus

Rosaceae

The raspberry was first cultivated in medieval monasteries. The fruits of wild raspberries are more nutritious than those of cultivated forms. Raspberries contain up to 13 per cent sugars, i. e. fructose, glucose, and saccharose, as much as 6 per cent pectins, cellulose, citric acid and the fever-reducing salicylic acid. They also contain up to 20 mg vitamin C per 100 g pulp, provitamin A, vitamins B_1 and B_2, also flavonoid glycosides, mucilages and iron, potassium, phosphorus, calcium and copper. Its considerable copper content is important in the formation of blood. Organic acids together with the seeds contained within the fruit help prevent constipation. The fruits which improve the digestion also have a diuretic effect and are recommended against rheumatism. At home you can use them in soups, desserts, salads, compotes, jams, syrups and juices. It is also possible to make wines and liqueurs from them. Raspberry leaves also have medicinal properties. They should be collected when the plant flowers, and are either dried carefully in the shade so that they do not lose their green colour, or they are fermented (see p. 96). They contain tannins, saccharides, flavones, up to 800 mg vitamin C per 100 g, organic acids and other substances. Tea can be made from them, often in combination with blackberry leaves and tops of sweet woodruff. This has diuretic effects, helps the body to secrete gall, improves digestion, and is a healthy substitute for real tea.

3

2

Description
Raspberry (1) is a perennial shrub which reaches a height of one and a half metres. The creeping root stem produces erect stems which arch at the top, become woody and start to branch in the second year. It grows throughout the

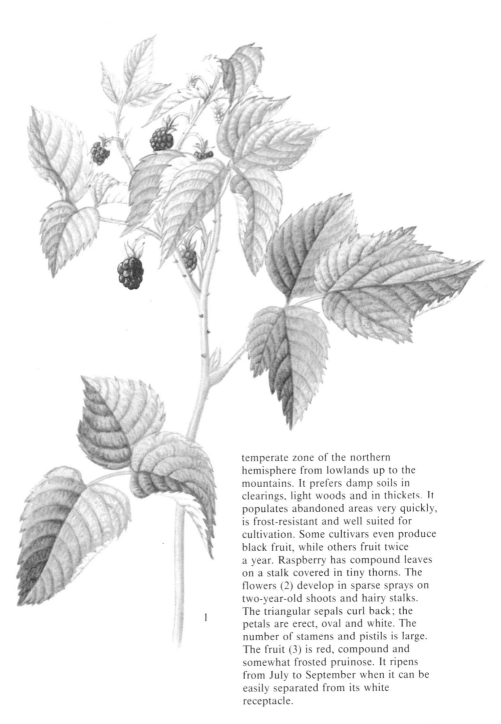

temperate zone of the northern
hemisphere from lowlands up to the
mountains. It prefers damp soils in
clearings, light woods and in thickets. It
populates abandoned areas very quickly,
is frost-resistant and well suited for
cultivation. Some cultivars even produce
black fruit, while others fruit twice
a year. Raspberry has compound leaves
on a stalk covered in tiny thorns. The
flowers (2) develop in sparse sprays on
two-year-old shoots and hairy stalks.
The triangular sepals curl back; the
petals are erect, oval and white. The
number of stamens and pistils is large.
The fruit (3) is red, compound and
somewhat frosted pruinose. It ripens
from July to September when it can be
easily separated from its white
receptacle.

Common Sorrel
Rumex acetosa
Polygonaceae

Common sorrel is the best known of all the sorrels we use as a vegetable. It grows throughout Europe, in the temperate zone of Asia, in
North America and Chile. Its young crisp leaves are collected early in
spring before the plant starts to flower. They are a source of valuable
substances; they contain about 14 per cent dry matter, 4 per cent proteins, 8 per cent saccharides, calcium, magnesium and iron. Vitamin
C is also present in a higher concentration than in lemons, about
50 mg per 100 g of fresh leaves. Common sorrel has a significant content of oxalic acid. It is for this reason that it should not be consumed
often and even not in large quantities — at the most 50—100 mg per
person. Dishes which contain it should be supplemented by milk,
cream or eggs, and should not be eaten by people who suffer from
kidney or gall stones. Sorrel leaves are, however, used in spring herb
cures. Due to their iron content they improve the formation of blood.
They also have mild diuretic effects, stimulate the appetite and regulate liver and gall-bladder activity. The leaves of sorrel are used in the
kitchen only in their fresh state as a supplementary vegetable or
spice, prepared in the same way as spinach. They are added finely
chopped to salads, sourly flavoured soups and sauces, mayonnaise,
soft cheese spreads and also grilled meats. They are traditionally
added to Russian borshch. In addition to the common sorrel, it is
possible to collect the leaves of sheep's sorrel. Other taller *Rumex*
species, such as great water dock (*R. hydrolapathum*) are not suitable
for eating. The cultivated forms of sorrel have mostly large, light
green leaves and a delicate, slightly sour flavour. Sorrel is easily cared
for and gives very good yields in fertile soil.

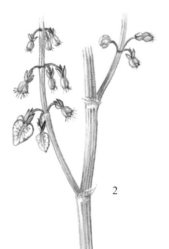

2

Description
Common sorrel (1) is a perennial herb
which reaches a height of about half
a metre. It is a widely distributed field
weed that can also be found in damp
meadows, pastureland and other grassy
places with a nitrogen-rich substrate,
from the lowlands up to a height of
2,000 metres above sea level. It has
a leafy stem, branched at the top, the

basal leaves slightly fleshy with deep, irregular lobes. They have long stalks, oblong to spear-shaped blades and are triangular at the base. The stem leaves have no stalks. The red-purple colouring of leaf stalks and stems is caused by the presence of a pigment antocyanogen. The bisexual, tiny, green to red flowers are arranged in clusters of up to 25 cms in length (2). They flower from May to August. The fruit is a small, dry seed pod (3). Sorrel also multiplies vegetatively by its roots. Reproduction by seed restricts the harvesting of the tops before the pods ripen.

Sheep's Sorrel
Rumex acetosella   Polygonaceae

Sheep's sorrel can be found in dry, less fertile soil than the common sorrel, which demands richer soils with a sufficient supply of nitrogen. However, it does have a similar use in the kitchen. Fresh, finely chopped leaves are used to give a sour flavour to soups, potato and vegetable salads, sauces, mayonnaise, spreads and to spice grilled meats. They can also be prepared like spinach. Sheep's sorrel, due to its oxalic acid content, should also be used in small quantities and not too frequently. The dishes should always be supplemented by dairy products, such as cottage cheese, milk, cheese, cream and yoghurt. Otherwise sheep's sorrel contains a number of very valuable substances. It has a relatively large vitamin C content, about 50 mg per 100 g, carotene, iron, manganese, potassium, silicon, some volatile oils, tannins and other substances. In the same way as comnon sorrel it stimulates digestion, improves appetite and assists in blood formation.

3

Veal with Sorrel

Ingredients
700 g veal, 2 tbsp butter, 10 small shallots, 1 glass of white wine, 1 cup of stock, 1 tsp cornflour, 100 g sorrel, 4 tbsp cream, salt, pinch of grated nutmeg

Method
Cube meat and fry in butter. Add whole shallots, salt and spice and fry a little longer. Add wine and braise until the meat is tender. Reduce meat juice to fat, add stock and thicken with cornflour mixed in a drop of water. Destalk clean sorrel and scald leaves with boiling water. Add leaves to meat and simmer for a short time. Finally, add cream and simmer for another 5 minutes on a low heat. Serve with boiled potatoes or white bread.

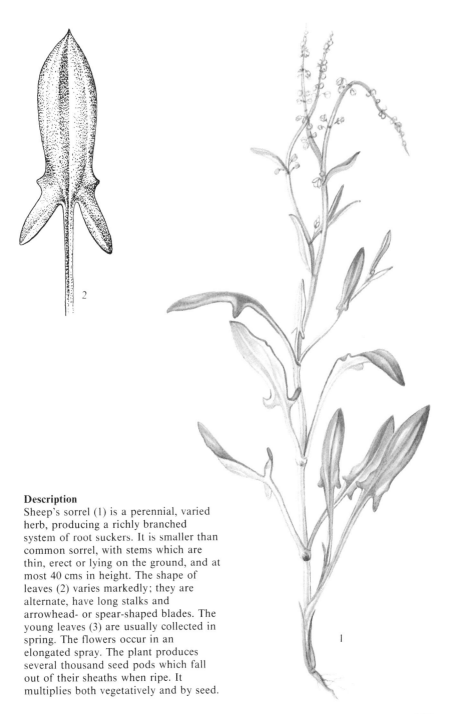

Description
Sheep's sorrel (1) is a perennial, varied
herb, producing a richly branched
system of root suckers. It is smaller than
common sorrel, with stems which are
thin, erect or lying on the ground, and at
most 40 cms in height. The shape of
leaves (2) varies markedly; they are
alternate, have long stalks and
arrowhead- or spear-shaped blades. The
young leaves (3) are usually collected in
spring. The flowers occur in an
elongated spray. The plant produces
several thousand seed pods which fall
out of their sheaths when ripe. It
multiplies both vegetatively and by seed.

173

Sage
Salvia officinalis
Labiatae

Sage was used as a spice in ancient times, particularly in the regions surrounding the Mediterranean Sea, where it is still one of the most popular herbs. It originated in the Mediterranean, where it grows on limestone rocks and screes. At present it is cultivated almost all over the world including Britain; in Europe its cultivation dates back to the Middle Ages. Its fresh and dried leaves are used as a herb. They are collected before or during flowering, ideally in dry conditions around midday, and are dried in a thin layer in the shade. They contain as much as 3 per cent volatile oil with camphor, also tannins, bitters, waxes, saponins, substances with hormonal effects, vitamins of the B group, so-called vitamin P and minerals etc. Sage is a beneficial, non-irritant spice and a healing herb. It has a strong aroma and a distinct, bitterish, spicy flavour and should be used only in small doses. Dried sage has a stronger effect than the fresh plant. For one portion, 1—2 fresh leaves or a pinch of dried, crushed leaves is sufficient. Sage goes best with lamb, pork, fish and tripe dishes. It goes well with mint, marjoram, parsley, basil and oregano, in stuffings, pâtés and forcemeats. Its fresh leaves are used as a stuffing for veal and pork, with grilled meats etc. and together with fresh parsley and hyssop adds a delicious aroma to herb butter. Sage has anti-inflammatory, antibacterial and antidiarrhoeal effects, it reduces perspiration and improves the activity of the gall-bladder. It is also used in cosmetics such as soaps and shampoos, in toothpastes and gargles to treat inflammation of the mouth and tonsillitis.

2

Description
Sage (1) is a perennial, profusely branching subshrub which grows to a height of 80 cms. The upper parts of its stems are herbaceous, often with a purple hue, the lower section woody. The leaves (2) are long ovals with serrated edges and a wrinkled upper surface, green-grey to silver-grey in colour. They emit a pleasant aroma when rubbed. Short lateral branches grow in the leaf joints and the flowers develop in groups of 5—10, forming sparse pseudowhorls (3). They appear from May to July on two-year old shoots and have short stalks,

3

4

a two-lipped calyx and a purple
corolla (4). The upper lip has two lobes
and two lower three, and the corolla
tube is lined with a ring of hair which
prevents unwelcome insects from
gaining access to the honey glands. Sage
is a much varied species, its cultivated
forms often reverting to the wild,
especially in vineyards.

1

175

Clary
Salvia sclarea
Labiatae

There are about 550 species of sage. Central Europe hosts six original and six introduced species. All sage species are very similar to each other but have different uses. Clary is native to southern Europe and may be cultivated in Britain by seed. Since it has lovely, conspicuous flowers accentuated by the coloured bracts, it is cultivated in gardens, from where it sometimes escapes into the open. Its flowers are collected for commercial use between July and August and for culinary use the leaves and tops in June, before flowering. The scent of the whole plant is reminiscent of lavender and geranium, being very strong, bitterish and very spicy. In the past, clary was used to spice wines in which other various aromatic and medicinal herbs were also steeped or boiled. This wine was then used for medicinal purposes. Nowadays this plant is used in the making of vermouths and dessert wines, alcoholic and nonalcoholic beverages and to spice vinegar. It also has an application in perfumery. Whenever its pleasant geranium-like flavour is suitable, for example in fruit soups, puddings and compotes and spiced baked vegetable dishes with meat, its leaves are used. Clary contains a volatile oil with sclareol, linalol and other ingredients, which give it a pleasant aroma. It also contains tannins, resins, bitter principles, vitamin C, provitamin A and minerals. In comparison with sage it does not have such strong medicinal effects. It is effective against spasms of the digestive tract, flatulence, sickness and diarrhoea. Externally, an infusion of clary can be used for bathing wounds.

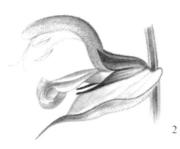

Description
Clary (1) is a biennial plant. In the first year it forms a basal rosette of leaves and a square, erect, slightly branching, leafy stem which reaches a height of one metre. The lower leaves are broadly oval, finely scalloped and wrinkled. The upper leaves have short stalks and blue to purple bracts. The flowers (2) which appear in the second year have five petals, are short-stalked with a broadly bell-shaped calyx; the corolla is pink to

2

purple, has a smooth tube and brownish
lower lip. The flowers develop in sparse
clusters in the joints of bracts; the whole
floral arrangement is very decorative.
The fruits are nutlets (3).

1

Elder
Sambucus nigra

Caprifoliaceae

The natural habitat extends throughout Europe and the Near East. The flowers are collected from May to July and its well-ripened fruits from August to September. The flowers and fruits have a high biological value. The flowers contain sugars, organic acids, flavonoid glycosides (3 per cent rutin etc.), tannins, amines, 350 mg of vitamin C per 100 g, traces of volatile oil, phytoncides etc. Before its preparation in the kitchen it is advisable to remove as many stalks as possible since they have an unpleasant smell and taste. The flowers are used in the making of syrups, wines, lemonades and carbonated drinks and can be also coated in egg batter and fried. Dried, they are used for making a medicinal tea. The flowers encourage perspiration and have anti-inflammatory, disinfective and mildly laxative effects. Fresh flowers are used in the preparation of an infusion at a ratio of one handful of flowers scalded with a $\frac{1}{2}$ litre boiling water to bathe an unhealthy, spotty complexion. The fruits contain sugars, organic acids, glycosides (sambunigrin), volatile oil, valuable antocyanic pigments, tannins, flavonoid glycosides (rutin), carotene, vitamin C and effective hormonal substances. They are used in the preparation of jams, compotes, juices, fruit soups and sauces, syrups, liqueurs, wines, fillings for tarts, soft cheese desserts etc., sometimes in combination with other fruits such as apples, pears or rowanberries. The fruits have a mild laxative effect and suppress neuralgic pains. They are also useful in slimming diets. For medicinal purposes the fruits are dried together with their stalks which are removed when drying is completed. NOTE: The berries should not be eaten raw. When preparing them, as many stalks as possible should be removed as they contain sambunegrin which irritates the kidneys and has diuretic effects.

2

Description
Elder (1) is a robust, spreading shrub or tree which reaches a height of up to six metres. It has a brown, cracked bark. Elders can be found growing along the edges of forests and fields, on rubbish dumps, along walls and in other places which have a sufficient supply of moisture and nitrogen. It can be found growing as a weed in parks. The leaves are opposite and compound, with irregularly serrated leaflets. The floral

1

arrangements are profuse, flat umbrella-shaped sprays. The flowers (2) are regular, five-petalled and yellowish white, with a strong, almost unpleasant smell. The composite fruit (3) is formed by tiny, spherical, red-purple, shiny berries. They have three seeds and a soft, staining flesh.

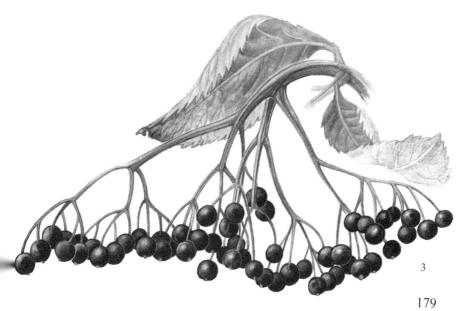

3

179

Winter Savory
Satureja montana
Labiatae

As early as the Third Century AD, the Latin cooking manual *'De re Coquinaria'* sang the praises of savory as a culinary herb. It reached central Europe probably in the 9th century and has been cultivated in gardens ever since the Middle Ages. It is native to the regions surrounding the Black Sea, from the eastern Mediterranean and southern Europe. Here it forms an integral part of the evergreen herbaceous cover. There are two savory species in existence, winter savory and summer savory (*S. hortensis*), both of which can be used in the kitchen. The tops, which are cut off during flowering from July to September, are dried in the shade in a draught and the dry leaves are subsequently rubbed off. They can also be used fresh. The whole plant is very aromatic and has a very sharp, peppery flavour. The most aromatic are the youngest topmost leaves. Savory should never be chopped as it then has a bitter taste. It contains up to 2 per cent volatile oil, up to 8 per cent tannins, mucilages, resins, antibacterial components, vitamin C, provitamin A, terpenes, bitter principles etc. It has antidiarrhoeal and antiflatulent effects, improves the appetite and digestion and it calms nausea. As a spice it goes well in dishes with a high fat content and those which may cause flatulence. It can be used as a substitute for those who cannot tolerate pepper. It is used to spice poultry, game, fish and other meats, cheeses, soups and dishes made from pulses, for example peas at a ratio of $\frac{1}{2}$ kg peas to two strong stems, in stuffings, minced meats, smoked meats, pickled vegetables and sauerkraut. It is also part of the Bulgarian spice mixture called 'chubritsa'.

Description
Winter savory (1) is a perennial, very aromatic subshrub reaching a height of 40 cms. The evergreen leaves occur in

pairs opposite each other and at right angles to the pair below. They are tiny, leathery and oval to spear-shaped in outline. Tiny, lipped flowers (2) with a bell-shaped calyx and light purple, pinkish to purple corolla are arranged in pseudowhorls. They open from July to September and are pleasantly aromatic. The fruits are tiny, dark brown nutlets. Summer savory (3) has fewer leaves then winter savory. They are narrow and spear-shaped. It is cultivated in gardens, from where it escapes to the wild.

1

3

Common Houseleek, Roof Houseleek
Sempervivum tectorum   Crassulaceae

The name of this fleshy-leafed plant originates from the medieval superstition that it protected houses against being struck by lightning. That is the reason why it used to be planted on the roofs (*tectum* = roof) and walls which undoubtedly it could not protect from lightning; nevertheless it decorated them and made them firmer with its roots. Even now many houseleek species adorn rockeries and dry walls in gardens. Houseleek's native regions are the foot of the Alps, the Pyrenees, the Massif Central in France and the northern part of the Balkans, and it grows at a height of about 800—1,000 metres above sea level. It easily reverts to the wild in Europe, so is often found in the open countryside. It inhabits dry locations, crumbling rocks and stone walls, where it forms thick covers. The young leaves are collected for both culinary and medicinal use. They can be gathered all year round but best of all at the beginning of the flowering season, as later they become coarse. They have a slightly sour taste, and can be used in salads dressed with vinegar, oil, salt and pepper. If 5—10 leaves are macerated for several hours in a glass of cold water, the resulting pleasant tasting drink is useful in cases of fever and catarrh. The houseleek is not often used in the kitchen. Its leaves contain sugars, mucilages, resin, bitter principles, organic acids, for example citric etc., tannins, vitamins and other substances. The juice from crushed leaves or the crushed leaves themselves can be used to dress swellings after insect bites, bunions, warts, freckles etc. or 1 tbsp of juice can be added to 1 $\frac{1}{2}$ glasses of water as a gargle to relieve inflammations of the mouth.

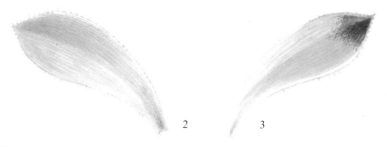

2   3

182

Description
Common houseleek (1) is a perennial herb which forms spreading basal rosettes of fleshy leaves (2) which are pointed, smooth, green and tinged red-brown on the outer tips (3). The mature rosettes produce, from June to August, whitish cottony stems (4) between 10 and 30 cms in height, with scaly leaves edged in long hair. The small, pink, star-shaped flowers are arranged in terminal monochasial sprays. When the plant stops flowering, the leaf rosette dies off. The fruits are follicles containing many seeds. However, it usually multiplies vegetatively by spherical rosettes which spread rapidly to produce large carpets.

4

1

183

Common Whitebeam
Sorbus aria
Rosaceae

The genus *Sorbus* covers about 90 species which grow in the temperate zone of the northern hemisphere. In the wild it is possible to find many natural crossbreeds of the individual species belonging to this genus, and also those of two related genera, for example crosses with the pear (*Sorbopyrus*), serviceberry (*Amelosorbus*) and chokeberry (*Sorbaronia*). These are usually deciduous shrubs or trees with simple or odd-numbered complex leaves with serrated edges and white or pink flowers in clusters. The fleshy fruits are similar to berries, and varied in size and colour. Whitebeam is a common species of deciduous forests, especially oak woods. It is widespread in central and southern Europe, reaching as far as the Altai and Himalaya and in the north to Sweden. The fruits, orange-red and fleshy, are similar in size to a small cherry and collected when fully ripe. They can be eaten only after being exposed to frost. They have an acrid taste and floury flesh, and contain a considerable amount of vitamin C, provitamin A, sugars, bitter principles, pectins, tannins, minerals, antocyanic pigment and other substances. They have slight diuretic and anti-inflammatory effects. When preserved in spirit, they can be used to help digestive disorders. They are also added to antisclerotic tea mixtures. They are not suitable for making juices, but can be used in the production of wines, liqueurs and also dried in tea for diabetics. The fruits of all *Sorbus* species contain sorbitol, a sweet alcohol which is easily absorbed by the body without raising the blood sugar level.

Description
Common whitebeam (1) is a tall shrub or a tree with a broad, pyramid-shaped or oval crown. It reaches a height of up to 10 metres. The leaves are stalked, broadly oval, elliptical, long, leathery, whitish tomentose beneath, with

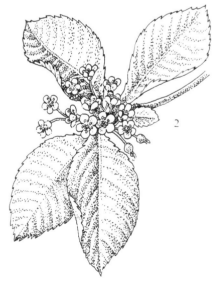

184

1

irregularly toothed edges and up to
12 cms in length. The flowers are small
and five-petalled, forming a terminal
cluster (2). They appear towards the end

of May and at the beginning of June.
The fruits (3) are fleshy, spherical, and
the same size as small cherries.
Whitebeam is related to *S. cretica* which
has smaller leaves, reaching up to only
7 cms in length. Whitebeam forms
several varieties, for example *aurea* with
yellow leaves, *edulis* with larger fruits, as
well as a number of crossbreeds.

185

Rowan, Mountain Ash
Sorbus aucuparia
Rosaceae

Rowan grows all over Europe as far as the polar forest limit. In Germanic mythology it was a sacred tree consecrated to the god Donar. The fruits are picked in September, in dry weather. Only red, perfect, fully ripe berries, should be used. They contain organic acids, i. e. malic, tartaric, and citric, as well as volatile parasorbic acid and sugars, particularly especially sorbit. In addition there are tannins, provitamin A in a strength of 48 mg per 100 g, bitter principles, vitamin C in about the same quantity as in lemons, volatile oil, flavonoid glycosides, i. e. rutin, quercetin etc. The fruits have mild laxative and diuretic effects, they slightly lower blood pressure and promote the formation of gall. They are therefore a suitable accompaniment for heavy dishes which are difficult to digest. The berries also contain parasorbic acid which irritates the kidneys; this changes into a non-toxic sorbic acid through drying or boiling. Despite this, rowanberries should still be consumed with restraint. They have a light apple-like aroma and a bitter and astringent taste. They are used in making compotes, syrups, ciders, liqueurs, jams, often with elderberries. They can also be dried; this should be done quickly, preferably by using artificial heat so that they keep their original colour. Dry fruits are used in tea or steeped in cold water — 1 tsp fruit to 2 glasses of cold water to produce a vitaminized, mildly laxative and diuretic beverage. They are also used in sauces to be served with game.

2

Description
Rowan (1) is a tree of up to 15 metres in height with an ovoid crown. It occurs from lowlands up to the mountain pine belt, and in the mountains up to a height of 1,600 metres above sea level. It is planted in avenues, in parks and gardens and its sweet-fruited varieties are cultivated as fruit trees. The most valuable is ssp. *moravica* which has larger fruits which do not have the bitter flavour. There are many crossbreeds of the genus *Sorbus* in existence. Rowan has a grey-brown bark which remains smooth for a long time. On old trees the bark peels off in smooth, paper-like

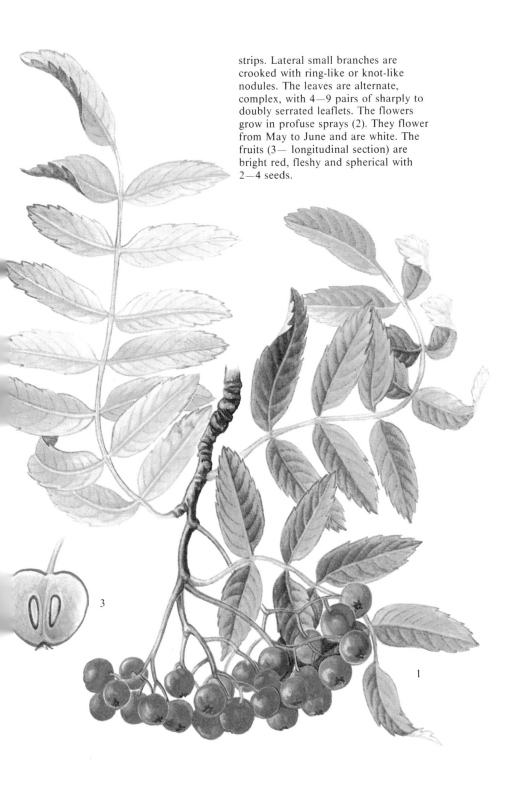

strips. Lateral small branches are
crooked with ring-like or knot-like
nodules. The leaves are alternate,
complex, with 4—9 pairs of sharply to
doubly serrated leaflets. The flowers
grow in profuse sprays (2). They flower
from May to June and are white. The
fruits (3— longitudinal section) are
bright red, fleshy and spherical with
2—4 seeds.

Rowan
Sorbus aucuparia ssp. *moravica*   Rosaceae

One of the sweet-fruited mutations of the rowan is *Sorbus aucuparia* ssp. *moravica*. It grows wild throughout Eurasia and in north-western Africa. It is a variable subspecies producing various forms and growing from lowlands as far as and beyond the upper forest limit. It is resistant to chemical air pollution and therefore can survive well in an urban environment. It grows in almost all soils but fruits best in nourishing and damp soils. The fruits are collected when fully ripe. They are larger than the fruits of other rowans with a better flavour and without the unpleasant astringent taste. They contain a large quantity of vitamins. 100 g fresh fruits contains as much as 550 mg vitamin C (in dried fruit up to 150 mg) and about 48 mg provitamin A. Furthermore the fruits contain sorbit, pectins, organic acids, bitter principles, tannins, pigments and saccharides. The fruits are seldom eaten fresh; they are usually processed or dried. The products from them retain a considerable amount of vitamins. Compotes are very tasty. The fruits can also be made into juices, syrups, preserves, liqueurs, wine, vinegar and brandy, and can also be candied. Dried and fresh rowanberries are added to sauces to be served with game or they can be used as a substitute for raisins. The dried berries are used in the preparation of medicinal, antisclerotic and vitaminized tea. They have anti-inflammatory, diuretic effects and stimulate the secretion of gall.

Description
Sorbus aucuparia ssp. *moravica* (1) is a tree with a cone-shaped, oval to spherical crown. The roots are branched, for the most part spread out at a depth of 30 to 40 cms under the ground surface. According to the environment it reaches a height of 7—15 metres and lives from 50 to 80 years. The leaves (2) are complex, with the leaflets serrated to only half of their length. They have white flowers which are arranged in a loose, irregular spray. They flower about 10 to 14 days later than apple trees. This rowan fruits regularly on two- or more-years-old branches. The fruits are small, red and fleshy, ripening according to the altitude from the end of August to mid-September. They do not fall when ripe, so can be collected as late as the arrival of frost.

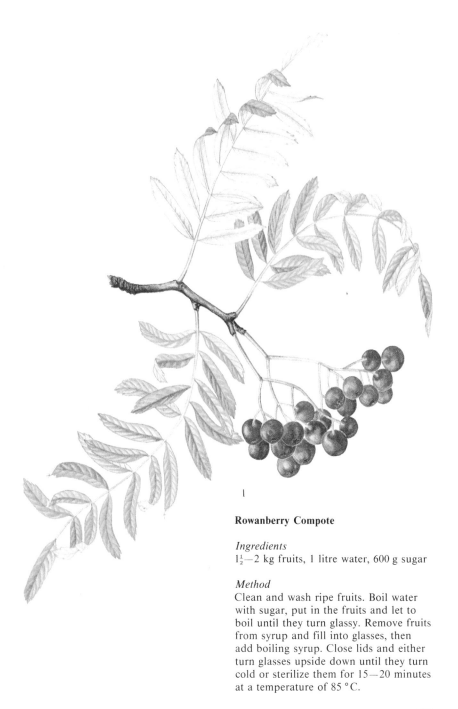

Rowanberry Compote

Ingredients
$1\frac{1}{2}$—2 kg fruits, 1 litre water, 600 g sugar

Method
Clean and wash ripe fruits. Boil water
with sugar, put in the fruits and let to
boil until they turn glassy. Remove fruits
from syrup and fill into glasses, then
add boiling syrup. Close lids and either
turn glasses upside down until they turn
cold or sterilize them for 15—20 minutes
at a temperature of 85 °C.

Service-tree
Sorbus domestica
Rosaceae

Ancient Romans are credited with introducing the service-tree to the wine-growing regions of Europe. It originates from the area around the Mediterranean Sea and from northern Africa. It is a relatively rare species, which grows individually in vineyards, along the edges of forests, on banks etc. It thrives best in warm regions in lime-rich soils but will grow even in very poor subsoils. Although it is a warmth-loving woody species, it is also resistant to frost. The fruits are picked at the end of September either by shaking off or collecting after having fallen. Two types of service-tree occur in the wild, namely var. *pyriformis* and var. *maliformis*. The fruits are tiny, weighing only up to 10 g. They contain dry matter, pectins, fruit acids, sugars, cellulose, provitamin A and vitamin C. The fresh fruits are not eaten. They have a very astringent taste, and therefore need to be left to season. If they are collected at the right time, they will keep if stored in a shallow layer until the end of November. They are processed into quality marmalades, wines, pure spirit and are dried.

Liqueur from Service-tree Berries

Ingredients
2 kg berries, 1 litre alcohol such as gin, 1 litre water, 1 kg sugar, sprig of vanilla, 10 crushed almonds

Method
Macerate fruits with vanilla and almonds in alcohol for a month. Strain, squeeze fruit and filter juice back to maceration. Mix, pour into bottles and leave 1—2 months to mature.

Description
The service-tree (1) has a fairly spreading crown, is long-lived and reaches a height of twenty metres. There are known fifty-year-old specimens in existence. The tree is characterized by its slow growth and is distinguished by its considerable vitality and ability to regenerate. The bark of the trunk is similar to that of a pear tree. In spring conspicuously large green sticky buds can be found on the ends of small branches. The leaves are complex, alternate, up to 18 cms in length and composed of up to 21 oval leaflets which are serrated at the apex. The leaflets may be up to 7 cms long. The Service-tree flowers at the end of May. The white-pink flowers form a loose spray and the fruits (2) are fleshy and ripen in the second half of September. They are bright yellow with a red patch on the surface and conspicuous brown pores. The fruit contains between two and four brown, rounded seeds.

2

1

Wild Service-tree
Sorbus torminalis
Rosaceae

Wild service-tree is a European species. It grows from hills to mountains in dry soil, occurring most frequently in oak and hornbeam forests. It is an ornamental tree suitable for parks and groups of trees in an urban environment. The fruits of the wild service-tree have been dried, preserved and used as a medicine or a spice from ancient times. They are less palatable than fruits of the Rowan, so are not eaten fresh, but can be left to freeze, even at home in the freezer. They are dried, preserved in spirit for a liqueur or are added to jams and marmalades to increase their vitamin value and make use of their pectin content. As do rowanberries, they contain a lot of vitamin C, provitamin A, sugars, fruit acids, pectin, tannins and bitter principles.

Description
Wild service-tree (1) is a robust shrub or a tree, 15—20 metres tall with twigs which are square, cottony when young, and glossy later. It occurs in various forms and crossbreeds, for example, with whitebeam. The leaves are green, lobed in the upper part, divided nearly to the midrib in the lower part and covered in short hairs beneath; their outline is broadly oval with between three and five pointed, sharply serrated

notches at the sides. White, five-petalled flowers are arranged in loose sprays. They have many stamens and an inferior ovary. They flower late, from mid-May to mid-June. The fruit (2) is spherical to elliptical and fleshy, brown with dark dots when fully ripe. Wild service-tree produces a high-quality wood, much valued for carving.

Liqueur from Fruits of Wild Service-tree

Ingredients
200 g fruits, 0.8 litre alcohol such as gin, $\frac{1}{2}$ litre water, 1 kg sugar, rind of $\frac{1}{2}$ lemon

Method
Fill a wide-necked bottle with fruits, add lemon rind, alcohol and $\frac{1}{2}$ litre boiled and cooled water. Close bottle and stand it in a warm place. Strain the liquid after eight to ten days, press fruit and add juice to maceration. Add sugar dissolved in 0.7 litre water. Bottle liqueur and leave to mature for two months.

2

1

Common Chickweed
Stellaria media
Stellariaceae

Chickweed is a tiny, but profusely widespread and stubborn weed. It grows very quickly, thriving in lighter soils throughout the entire temperate zone of both hemispheres from low-lying to submountainous altitudes. It occurs in gardens, vegetable plots and other cultivated areas. Despite all the trouble it causes as a weed, it can be made into some very tasty dishes. The young crisp tops with their leaves are edible and are suitable for salads and soups. As well as being a source of vitamin C and having medicinal qualities, it contains glycosides, tannins and saponins. In folk medicine it is used as a tonic for those convalescing from tuberculosis. The crushed tops are used externally to dress wounds and eczemas. It has mild diuretic effects and is used to treat gout and rheumatism. It is used as fodder for cattle, also improving lactation in cows. Its young shoots can be collected practically all year round, even during a mild winter.

Mushroom Soup with Chickweed

Ingredients
1 ½ litres water, handful of fresh mushrooms, 2 potatoes, 1 onion, 3 tbsp barley, 2 cloves of garlic, 1 cup of chopped chickweed, pepper, chives, salt, cream (optional).

Method
Boil mushrooms, barley, cubed potatoes and sliced onion in water. Add crushed garlic and chickweed, also salt and pepper, bring soup to boil and set aside. Finally add chives and cream if desired.

2

3

Description

Chickweed (1) is an annual, overwintering or even biennial plant, which multiplies by seed and also vegetatively. Even the smallest piece of stem is capable of rooting on its own. Chickweed can form a very thick carpet within a short period of time. It is frost-resistant and flowers even in winter. It produces a square, creeping, branched, fragile stem up to 50 cms in length, which roots at its nodules. The leaves are small, narrow and spear-shaped. The flowers (2) are tiny and white but sometimes do not develop petals at all (3).

1

Common Dandelion
Taraxacum officinale   Compositae

The common dandelion is one of the most common spring salad vegetables. It grows profusely almost all over Europe from the Arctic region to the mountains of the subtropics. It is a considerably varied
species; in Europe alone it is possible to find some one thousand subspecies and varieties, all difficult to differentiate from one another.
Apart from the wild forms which grow in the countryside, cultivated
varieties, all difficult to differentiate from one another. Apart from
the wild forms which grow in the countryside, cultivated varieties
also exist, with a larger root and more tender, slightly curled leaves.
Dandelion has been cultivated as a vegetable since the 17th century
and is most popular in France, Germany and Italy. The entire plant,
which freely exudes a milky sap, is collected. The leaves and roots of
wild plants are harvested before the plant starts to flower. Dandelion
leaves contain 50 mg of vitamin C per 100 g, vitamins of the B group,
2 mg of provitamin A in 100 g, i. e. about the same as carots, choline,
saponins and glycosides. They also contain potassium, sodium, aluminium, manganese, copper, iron, calcium, sulphur and phosphorus.
The roots especially contain a bitter taraxacin, tannins, resins and inulin; because of this dandelion roots are particularly suitable for people suffering from diabetes. Substances contained in the leaves assist
the metabolism, lower blood pressure and secretion of gall and urine.
They are also recommended for gout and rheumatism. The flowers
are used to loosen congestion. In the kitchen, young leaves in particular are used. The younger they are, the tastier and more delicate.
However, it is best to blanch the leaves as this dispels their bitterness.
They are mostly prepared as salads, but in smaller quantities they are
added to spring herb soups and sauces or are cooked in the same way
as spinach. The roots can be boiled and also added to salads, and the
flowers are used in the making of syrup and wine.

Description
The common dandelion (1) is
a profusely widespread perennial herb.
The short root stem with its scaly
remnants of dead leaves produces
a fleshy taproot. Damaged areas freely
emit a white, bitter sap. The leaves,
which are simple, longitudinally
lanceolate, saw-toothed with lobes
curved towards the base, and narrowing
into a broad stalk form a basal rosette.
From this rise hollow cylindrical scapes
terminated in a flower head which
consists of about two hundred
strap-shaped, bisexual, yellow florets (2).
Dandelions flower in large numbers in
May. In summer and autumn they
flower again, although less profusely.

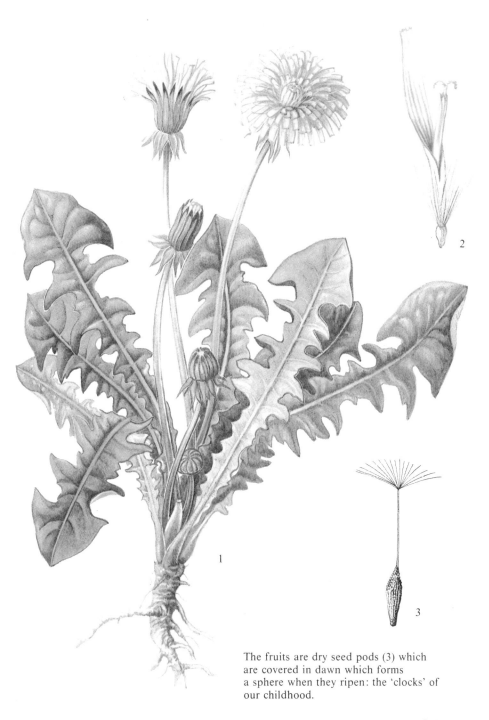

The fruits are dry seed pods (3) which
are covered in dawn which forms
a sphere when they ripen: the 'clocks' of
our childhood.

197

Wild Thyme, Breckland Thyme
Thymus serpyllum   Labiatae

Wild thyme varies greatly in form and chemical makeup and is composed of a large number of smaller species. They grow in the temperate zone of Eurasia as far as Siberia. About ten species and approximately twenty crossbreeds grow in Europe alone. They are all utilized as healing and culinary plants. The tops are collected shortly before or during flowering, when the plant has the largest quantity of volatile oil. They are snipped off with scissors and dried quickly in the shade. Since wild thyme is slowly diminishing in the wild it is important to take care when collecting it that the roots are not damaged and a part of the flowering stems remain intact. The plant contains a number of effective medicinal substances; particularly volatile oils, up to 1 per cent, which have a significant disinfective effect. Furthermore there are tannins, bitter principles, terpenes, flavonoid glycosides, vitamins, phytoncides, mineral substances etc. Wild Thyme regulates digestion, and is also effective for treating coughs and hoarseness. It is taken as an infusion of 1 tbsp crushed herb per cup, 3 times a day. When treating illnesses arising from the common cold, the tea can be sweetened with honey. It is also applied in medicinal cosmetics as a herbal bath, in creams and mouth rinses for its deodorant qualities. As a spice it is used in the production of gastric liqueurs, for example the well-known chartreuse. Wild thyme is used in cooking either fresh or dried, just like garden thyme and marjoram. It is good for dishes which are more difficult to digest and may cause flatulence. It has a pleasant, bitterish spicy flavour and a typical aroma. It improves the digestion and appetite and it can be used to spice soups, vegetable dishes, roasts, braised meats, baked dishes, sauces, omelets, stuffings, pulses etc. A mere pinch of wild thyme per portion is sufficient.

Description
Wild thyme (1) is a perennial herb or subshrub, partly creeping and partly ascending, downy, reddish, woody below and up to 20 cms tall. It can be found on dry, sunny slopes, banks, pastureland and alongside tracks. It is an important plant in the production of honey. Its tiny leaves are arranged in opposite pairs, at right angles to each other, oval and usually hairy beneath.

2

Purple or pale pink flowers (2) are
arranged in pseudowhorls (3); the calyx
is bell-shaped, downy and has five tips;
the corolla is two-lipped. The fruits are
nutlets.

3

1

Garden Thyme
Thymus vulgaris

Labiatae

Garden Thyme has been a well-known healing plant and spice since ancient times. Ancient Egyptians obtained from it a volatile oil for embalming mummies. In central Europe garden thyme started to be cultivated by Benedictine monks around the 11th century. It grows wild in the Western Mediterranean, especially in Spain, France and Italy, where it forms a part of the evergreen carpet covering rocky slopes. It is an introduced species in Britain. A number of cultivars with differently scented volatile oils such as lemon are cultivated in central Europe. It can also be grown in the rockery. The tops are collected at the beginning of the flowering season from May to June and for a second time in August and September. Garden Thyme is a spice but it also has medicinal properties. It contains up to 3 per cent volatile oil with tymol, carvacrol and other components, tannins, organic acids, bioflavonoids, bitter principles, saponins and substances with disinfective and anticonvulsive effects. As a spice garden thyme influences the secretion of gall; it soothes gastric and intestinal disorders and is effective against diarrhoea. As a culinary herb, garden thyme is used to spice meat stock, piquant sauces, fish, roast duck, game, veal and rabbit. It is used in smoked meats, forcemeats, pâtés and cheeses and also goes well with pulses, pizzas and vegetable dishes. Thyme should always be used with care as it is slightly bitter and very aromatic. Between one and two tsp of dry thyme for 1 kg food, otherwise only a sprig or a pinch of fresh leaves is sufficient. Thyme salt made from ground thyme and kitchen salt can be prepared for seasoning dishes. A pinch of thyme can be added to honey to sweeten tea taken when suffering from common cold. A branch of fresh thyme dipped in oil can be used to brush barbecued meat. Thyme is a component of a number of spice mixtures.

2

Description
Garden thyme (1) is a perennial subshrub which grows to a height of between ten and thirty cms and related to wild thyme. Entirely downy, herbaceous shoots grow from woody branches which are erect in their lower parts. The leaves are opposite each other in pairs and at right angles to those

above and below them, decussate, tiny, oval to linear. Clusters of tiny leaves often develop in the leaf joints. The flowers (2) are crowded in groups of 3—6 in the joints of the upper leaves. They form sparse sprays (3). The calyx is bell-shaped, five-toothed and two-lipped; the corolla is also two-lipped and white or pale purple to purple. The stigma is two-lobed.

3

1

201

Water Chestnut
Trapa natans
Trapaceae

Even as late as the 18th century the fruits of this aquatic plant, known as 'water nuts' or 'water chestnuts' played a considerable role in Europe's food supply. Water nuts are an old foodstuff which, along with hazel-nuts, were found in neolithic pile dwellings in Switzerland. In storage pits dating from the bronze age stores of them were discovered in layers up to 30 cms high. Probably because of their starch, protein and fat content, the fruits of the Water Chestnut were particularly important foodstuff in winter. They were also known in ancient Rome and in the Middle Ages they were even cultivated. These days they have their place in Chinese and Indian cuisine and are also used in Japanese, South African and Sinhalese dishes. In southern Europe they are used as fodder for pigs, and in some places are used in the making of decorative objects, rosaries, bracelets and necklaces. They are also available in Britain. The fruits of water chestnut have a firm, chocolate-brown casing which has an unusual, prickly shape. Inside is a nut, which can be eaten raw, boiled, roasted or ground into flour. Its flavour is similar to that of the edible chestnut. Today water chestnut can be found in the warm low-lying regions of the temperate zone and in the subropics of Europe and Asia. It grows in sunny places in swamps, shallow stagnant waters and blind river arms.

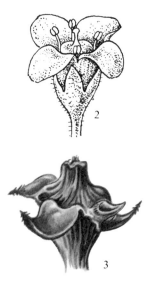

Chinese salad

Ingredients
200 g soya shoots or finely chopped cabbage, 200 g peas, 100 g water chestnuts, 2 onions, 150 g ham, 3 tbsp soya sauce, 1 tbsp white wine, pinch of ground ginger, pinch of sugar, 2—3 tbsp oil, 1 lettuce, salt, chives

Method
Fry chopped onion in oil, add chopped water chestnuts, soya shoots or cabbage and peas and braise briefly. Add thinly sliced ham and set aside. Flavour salad with soya sauce, wine, ginger, sugar and salt, sprinkle with chives and chill. Serve salad in a bowl lined with lettuce leaves.

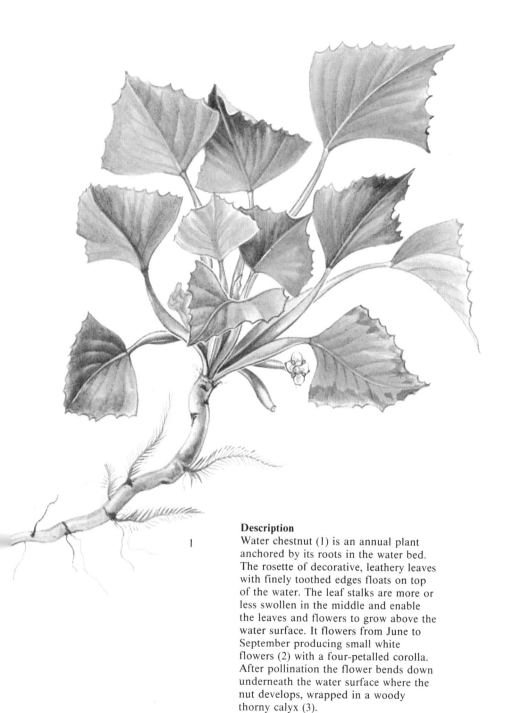

Description
Water chestnut (1) is an annual plant anchored by its roots in the water bed. The rosette of decorative, leathery leaves with finely toothed edges floats on top of the water. The leaf stalks are more or less swollen in the middle and enable the leaves and flowers to grow above the water surface. It flowers from June to September producing small white flowers (2) with a four-petalled corolla. After pollination the flower bends down underneath the water surface where the nut develops, wrapped in a woody thorny calyx (3).

Colt's-foot
Tussilago farfara

Colt's-foot grows almost throughout Europe, western Asia, the mountains of north-western Africa and has been introduced to North America. The young leaves and flower heads are edible and at the same time healing. The flowers contain volatile oil, yellow pigment, mucilage, tannins, bitter principles etc. The leaves also contain mucilage, bitter principles up to 15 per cent, tannins, organic acids, dextrin, inulin, saponin tussilagin, carotene and a number of vitamins, mainly C. They also contain a considerable amount of potassium and zinc. Colt's-foot soothes irritated upper respiratory passages, and is useful for the relief of coughs and asthma. Colt's-foot tea has been used to treat coughs since ancient times. It is often used in a mixture with other herbs, for example equal parts of colt's-foot, mullein and primrose. It is used to treat gastric catarrhs, high blood pressure and hardening of the arteries. Fresh crushed leaves can be used as a dressing for wounds, burns and sore rheumatic joints. For culinary purposes, the flowers are either dried and used for teas or they are in the preparation of medicinal honey and syrup. The leaves have a gluey, slightly bitter taste and can be used to add flavour to stuffed meat rolls or in a mixture with other herbs for soups and salads. They are used mainly in Japanese cuisine.

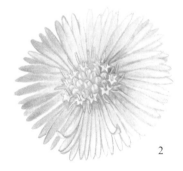

Description
Colt's-foot (1) is a perennial herb which spreads quickly by its branched creeping root stem. It is an important plant in infertile soils but at the same time also a difficult weed. It grows in areas from lowlands to mountains in damp clay soils, especially on secondary excavated and transferred subsoils such as quarries, landslide areas, banks etc. Early in spring stalks covered with red-brown scales grow from the flower buds. They bear a single pale yellow flower head (2) with strap-shaped female ray florets and male tubular disc

florets. They close in rainy weather and in the evening. The long-stalked basal leaves (3) start to grow only after the flower head has faded and the seeds have ripened. They have a rounded heart-shaped blade with a shallow toothed edge, which splits into 5—12 lobes. When young the leaves are densely white felted on both sides. The fruits are seed pods with glossy white down on the tips.

3

1

Common Nettle
Urtica dioica
Urticaceae

Nettles, familiar perennial weeds which grow in places with a sufficient amount of nitrogen in the soil, have been used as healing plants
and as a spring vegetable in the kitchen ever since ancient times. They
grow almost all over the world with the exception of the tropical regions of Africa and South America. The common nettle is a varied
species; some subspecies for instance lack the stinging hairs. For
kitchen use it is best to collect the youngest shoots in April and May
and later only the young tips and leaves. They are eaten cooked or
scalded with boiling water. The nettle hairs contain a toxic substance,
which disintegrates into harmless components at 85 °C. Nettle leaves
have a great nutritional value. They contain a large amount of chlorophyll and up to 100 mg vitamin C per 100 g, tannins, glucocinins
(which cause the blood sugar level to drop), acetic and formic acids,
B vitamins, provitamin A, histamine, cellulose, phytoncides, calcium,
potassium, iron, phosphorus and magnesium etc. The dried leaves
contain as much as 20 per cent protein and about 2 per cent fats. Nettle is a valuable medicinal herb which encourages metabolic activity,
regulates digestion, has diuretic effects and also stimulates the secretion of gall. Fresh juice from its leaves is often used in spring cures.
The fresh and dried tops can also be used as an infusion for washing
the hair. Nettles are also used in tea mixtures, soups, omelets and can
be cooked in the same way as spinach. They may be added to stuffings, especially at Easter, salads, scrambled eggs, minced meats,
spreads and fillings for savoury desserts.

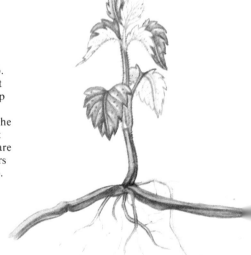

Description
Common nettle (1) is a perennial herb.
The richly branched underground root
stem spreads over large areas; in damp
forests the plant often forms vast
colonies. It has been introduced into the
vicinity of human habitation. The root
stems produce leaf stems that are square
and densely covered with stinging hairs
and may reach a height of 120 cms (2).
They branch after being cut.
The leaves are opposite,

206

elongated ovals with pointed tips and coarse serrated edges and are also covered with stinging hairs.The spike-like sprays of flowers are borne in the joints of the upper leaves. The female flower head is longer, pendent during the flowering season, and the male one is erect; the flowers are small and green. Nettles have a very complicated method of pollination; they rarely form fruits. Most frequently they multiply vegetatively, so eradication is very difficult.

Small Nettle
Urtica urens

Urticaceae

In contrast to its more robust perennial relative, the common nettle, small nettle is an annual weed. It germinates early in spring at low temperatures of about 0 °C and if it has favourable conditions, grows quickly. The youngest plants are collected as a vegetable or green spice early in spring. They are picked later than the common nettle, which overwinters and produces shoots from its creeping rootstocks. It is not advisable to pick excessively developed individuals because there is a danger that they will contain too many nitrates. The nettle tops contain proteins, fats, sugars, calcium, iron, organic acids, tannins, flavonoid glycosides, phytoncides, a large amount of vitamin C, provitamin A, chlorophyll and other substances the same as the common nettle. These encourage metabolic activity and the formation of blood cells, are effective in treating inflammations of the urinary tract and are supportive in the treatment of diabetes and rheumatism. Before preparing nettles in the kitchen they must be washed well and briefly scalded with boiling water so that they lose their stinging property. They are used in the preparation of soups and spinach and may be added to potato salads, stuffings, egg dishes, forcemeats etc. Young nettles are an excellent fodder for domestic farm animals.

Description
Small nettle (1) is an annual herb reaching a height of between 20 and 60 cms. In overall terms it is less robust than common nettle and can be reliably recognized by its single taproot and smaller leaves (2). The leaves (3) are opposite with oval blades and toothed edges. It is unisexual with male and female florets arranged in erect flower heads on the same plant. Usually male flowers are present in a greater number. One plant forms up to one thousand seed pods, which germinate in spring after the soil has been frozen. They maintain their power of germination for several years.

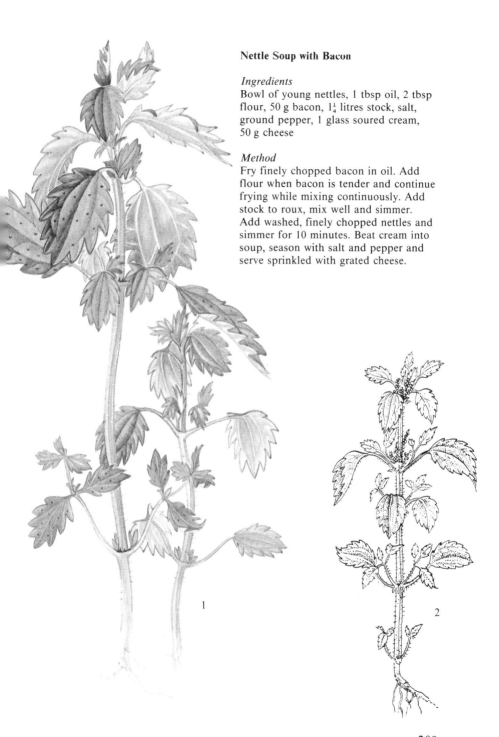

Nettle Soup with Bacon

Ingredients
Bowl of young nettles, 1 tbsp oil, 2 tbsp
flour, 50 g bacon, 1¼ litres stock, salt,
ground pepper, 1 glass soured cream,
50 g cheese

Method
Fry finely chopped bacon in oil. Add
flour when bacon is tender and continue
frying while mixing continuously. Add
stock to roux, mix well and simmer.
Add washed, finely chopped nettles and
simmer for 10 minutes. Beat cream into
soup, season with salt and pepper and
serve sprinkled with grated cheese.

1

2

Bilberry
Vaccinium myrtillus Ericaceae

Bilberries can be found all over Europe, particularly at high altitudes in poor acid soils. They thrive in sparse coniferous and deciduous forests, on the moors and pastureland. They also grow in north Asia and north-western America. The fruits, blue frosted berries, ripen in July and August. They are one of the most nutritious fruits. They contain tannins, citric and malic organic acids, pectins, sugars, anthocyanic pigment, glycosides, B vitamins, provitamin A and about 15 mg vitamin C per 100 g, calcium, potassium, iron and phosphorus. They are low in calories and, because of their disinfectant nature, effective in healing inflammations of the mouth. Dried bilberries are effective and harmless in the treatment of diarrhoea. Fresh bilberries with sugar and milk, on the other hand, have a mild laxative effect. They also lower the blood sugar level and the pigment present in them assists in the regeneration of the magenta in the eye. Bilberries can be used in juices, syrups, wine, compotes, jams, desserts, fruit soups, sauces, and can also be frozen. The dried leaves are also used in medicine. They are picked from May to August, rubbed off carefully from the branches to avoid harming the plant. They contain many tannins, glucocins which lower the blood sugar level, organic acids, flavonoid glycosides etc. They have antidiarrhoeal and anti-inflammatory effects, and an infusion from the leaves may be used as a gargle to treat mouth inflammations.

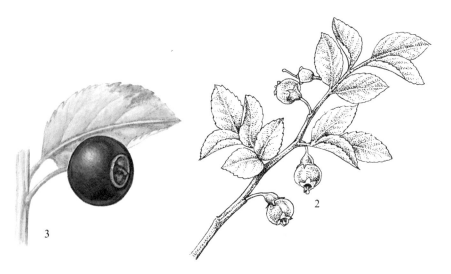

1

Description

Apart from its valuable fruits, the bilberry (1) also has great ecological importance. It protects forest floors from erosion and helps to form humus, forming a network of roots and creeping root stems which produce erect, square, profusely branched small stems, covered by a thin grey bark in their oldest parts.

Young branches are green. The deciduous leaves are opposite, short-stalked, and have finely scalloped edges. Individual reflexed flowers (2) develop on stalks in leaf joints. The calyx is indistinct with 4—5 small, blunt teeth. The pitcher-shaped corolla is coloured whitish- or pinkish-green with a long protruding stigma. The fruit (3) is a spherical berry, which looks as though it is cut off at the top, with a remnant of the calyx and thread-like stigma. Large-fruited bilberries originating from the United States are cultivated in gardens. Their fruits are used in a similar way to forest bilberries. They belong to another botanical species, most frequently *V. corymbosum*.

211

Cranberry
Vaccinium oxycoccus
Ericaceae

Cranberry is a small evergreen shrub related to cowberry. It occurs in smaller numbers in the wild but in some areas of Europe, e. g. in Siberia, it is considerably widespread and is an important source of fruits. It grows in Europe, Asia and North America. The fruits ripen in September but are collected after the first frosts or in spring. In Tsarist Russia, the leaves of both cranberries and raspberries were used for making tea. The fruits of the cranberry are used in the same way as those of the cowberry. They have a sour acrid taste, but their flavour improves once they have been frozen. They contain about 2.5 per cent saccharides and 2—3 per cent organic acids such as citric, benzoic, and quinic. Due to their benzoic and quinic acid content the fruits and products made of them have a long shelf life. They contain about 15 mg vitamin C per 100 g pulp, also the glycosides vacciniine and ericoline, tannins, pectin, anthocyanic pigments and trace elements, for example iodine. They are made into preserves, juices, syrups and compotes, and can also be frozen or preserved in honey. They are used in the preparation of a sauce to be served with game or poultry, in the same way as cowberries. In Siberia they are used to spice sauerkraut. The juice from cranberries is used in folk medicine to treat sore throats and the common cold, and tea made from the leaves is taken for diseases of the urinary and gall tracts, for rheumatism, gout and to treat diarrhoea.

Description
Cranberry (1) is a perennial subshrub with slender creeping stems and ascending branches. It grows in acid heath soils, on moors with an excess of water or in wet meadows and forests. It has short-stalked alternate, leathery, small leaves with curled edges (2 — underside of the leaf). The flowers (3) grow in groups of two or three on long stalks. They have a pink corolla, the petals curl back soon after opening and there are eight to ten stamens. The fruit (4) is a spherical to oval, red to dark red, occasionally white berry. The related large cranberry (*V. macrocarpum*) has larger fruits and grows wild in North America. It has been developed and over two hundred varieties are cultivated in the United States, Canada and Holland on plantations, especially on exhausted moorland with a high water table. It is used in the same way as the cowberry.

1

2

3

4

213

Cowberry
Vaccinium vitis-idaea
Ericaceae

The cowberry grows in dry acid forest soils with a sufficient supply of humus and on the moors from lowlands to the mountains. In the Alps it has been found at a height of three thousand metres above sea level. It is widespread throughout Europe, mainly in northern regions, reaching beyond the polar circle, in Asia as far as Japan and in North America. Cowberries are very popular fruit, white at first, later a vivid red, glossy, bitter to sour and floury. They ripen gradually from June to September and should be collected when fully ripe. They contain sugars, citric and malic acids and in smaller quantities also benzoic and oxalic acids, flavonoid glycosides, tannins, vegetable pigments, and glycosides arbutin and vaccinin which is effective in cases of inflammation of the urinary tract. They contain also pectin, provitamin A, about 20 mg vitamin C per 100 g, manganese and many other minerals. The fruit improves digestion and appetite and is effective against diarrhoea. The juice also lowers fever accompanying infectious diseases. Cowberries are not recommended for people who suffer from kidney stones because of their oxalic acid content. They should not be eaten raw, but are made into jams and sauces and compotes, which are best served with game, especially venison, pheasant and partridge. They are also dried and added to game and sirloin with cream sauce. Preserved cowberries do not deteriorate since they contain a natural preservative, benzoic acid, in quantities harmless to human health. A decoction from cowberry leaves is used to treat diarrhoea, kidney and urinary tract inflammations and as a supportive treatment of diabetes.

2

Description
Cowberry (1) is a low subshrub. The creeping, branched root stem produces arched to ascending branches. The non-deciduous leaves are alternate, short-stalked, oval, thick and leathery.

The flowers, grouped in semi-pendent
bunches (2), develop at the tips of
branches. They are white to light pink in
colour, have a faint scent and open in
June and July. The fruits are berries
which change colour as they ripen from
green to white, finally turning a vivid
red. They contain black seeds.

1

Lamb's Lettuce, Common Cornsalad
Valerianella locusta
Valerianaceae

Lamb's lettuce is an original European species, native to the Mediterranean. It grows wild throughout the temperate zone of Europe, in the Near East, in the Caucasus, northern Africa and North America. It is a tasty spring salad vegetable, particularly nutritious in early spring. The leaves or the whole leaf rosettes without the root are cut off with a knife at the end of March, in April or in the autumn. They have a pleasant, slightly nutty flavour. Lamb's lettuce has a high nutritional content, greater than lettuce. It contains about 60 mg vitamin C, almost twice as much as lemons. It also has a large amount of phosphorus, calcium and iron, saccharides, proteins, fats etc. It improves the digestion and has a calming influence on the nervous system, and is useful as a spring tonic. Lamb's Lettuce is used only fresh in mixed and potato salads, in herb soups, omelets and spreads. Salad prepared from Lamb's Lettuce is very delicate, therefore the plants must not be squashed as they may lose their refreshing juiciness.

Description
Lamb's lettuce (1) is a small annual herb. It grows in wheat fields, uncut lawns, ditches, on pastureland from lowlands to submountain regions. It is an overwintering plant which germinates in the autumn and overwinters as a leaf rosette. It is undemanding and therefore . is suitable for gardens; it has been improved and cultivated into varieties with larger, more fleshy leaves. The basal rosettes of wild-growing plants (2) are only several centimetres high. They develop within a short period of time. The leaves (3) are elongated, with the typical network of ribs. The stems (4 — cross section) are 20—30 cms tall and forked. They are terminated in inconspicuous, small, bluish to white, crowded flowers.

Salad from Lamb's Lettuce and Flat Lettuce

Ingredients
1—2 heads of flat lettuce, a bowl of lamb's lettuce, 1 onion, 1 carton plain yoghurt, 50 g ham, 2 boiled eggs, 2 tbsp grated horseradish, a pinch of castor sugar, lemon juice, salt, 1 tbsp oil

Method
Wash flat lettuce and lamb's lettuce and break into small pieces. Add thinly sliced onion. Prepare a dressing from sugar, salt, yoghurt, oil, lemon juice and horseradish and pour over lettuce. Mix salad and decorate with finely chopped ham and sliced eggs.

216

217

Guelder-rose
Viburnum opulus
Caprifoliaceae

Guelder-rose is considered to be a shrub of life, youth and beauty. Its fruits are edible after being frozen, either in the freezer or having been left on the shrub until the first frosts. This results in their losing their acrid bitter taste. It is not recommended that they be eaten in large quantities. They contain pectin, saccharides, organic acids, tannins, carotene, more vitamin C than lemons, vitamin P, saponins, red pigment, the bitter principle viburnin, phytoncides etc. They are used in the preparation of compotes, juices, syrups, preserves and sauces to be served with meat dishes. The frozen fruits can be added to desserts, often in a mixture with other fruit. In the food industry the bright red, non-toxic pigment from guelder-rose fruits is used to colour alcoholic and soft drinks. The fruits have been employed in folk medicine since the 16th century. They are effective against cramp and have a calming effect. The juice from fresh or tea from dried fruits sweetened with honey is recommended in the treatment of the common cold, coughs, asthma, diarrhoea and gastric disorders. The fruits have a mild diuretic and phytoncidic effect and the juice from the fruits is recommended as an external cosmetic preparation to treat an unhealthy complexion. The bark also has healing properties. An alcohol extract can be used to ease menstrual pain.

Description
The shrub or tree of the guelder-rose (1) reaches a height of up to five metres. It is distributed throughout Europe and in the north reaches the boundary of the polar forest. It grows in thickets, along forest margins close to water, predominantly in damp to wet soils. It thrives up to a height of one thousand metres above sea level. The sterile form is planted out in parks and gardens for its ornamental value. The leaves of the guelder-rose are opposite, broadly oval, three- to five-lobed, with coarsely serrated edges. The flowers, which open in May and June, are arranged in terminal, profusely branched spherical clusters. The margins are formed by large white sterile flowers and in the middle there are small fertile flowers. The inner flowers (2) are bisexual, white or reddish. The corolla is globe-shaped with five teeth and there are five stamens. The fruit is round, bright red, fleshy and glossy with one seed (3).

1

3

219

Sweet Violet
Viola odorata
Violaceae

Sweet violet is one of the oldest medicinal plants. Ancient physicians credited it with great medicinal powers. It was used by Hippocrates, and Pliny the Elder recommended smelling the scent of the flowers to ease headache. Its healing properties are not really recognized these days. However, the volatile oils from the flowers are still amongst the most important components of perfumes. Sweet violet originates from western Europe, the Mediterranean and the Near East, and has been introduced to other parts of Europe. It is a much varied species. There are altogether about four hundred species of violets, of which more than thirty grow in Europe. Its young leaves are edible and are collected early in spring as soon as they start to bud. The same applies to the flowers and the flowering stems. The leaves can be added to herb soups, omelets etc. in combination with other spring herbs. The whole plant contains mainly saponins but also traces of a volatile oil which lowers blood pressure. It also contains salicylic acid and mucilages; the flowers contain a volatile oil, anthocyanic blue pigment, mucilages, flavonoid glycosides, malic acid, vitamins, sugar and other substances. It has expectorant properties and lessens stubborn coughs which accompany diseases of the upper respiratory tract. The flowers were once candied and taken to treat the common cold and cough. They are also used in the production of a syrup to cure coughs and insomnia and in the making of an aromatic vinegar. The root stem also has medicinal properties.

2

Description
Sweet violet (1) is a perennial herb with a short root stem and creeping runners growing in and above the ground. It is 10—20 cms tall. It grows quite profusely in shady groves, thickets, on grassy banks and alongside fences from lowlands to submountainous regions. Its cultivated forms often revert to the wild. The leaves (2) are in a basal rosette. When young they are furled like

a cornet. They have long stalks, are finely downy and heart- to kidney-shaped. Individual flowers (3) grow from the joints of the basal leaves on square stalks, which bend downwards into a hook at the ends. Halfway along the length of the stem there are opposite bracts. The sweet violet flowers, which are usually infertile, appear in March and April. In August and September the runners produce just at ground level inconspicuous flowers which do not open out and are self-pollinated. The fruit (4) is a three-valved capsule with numerous seeds. Sweet violet is similar to many other violet species, the leaves and flowers of which are also edible.

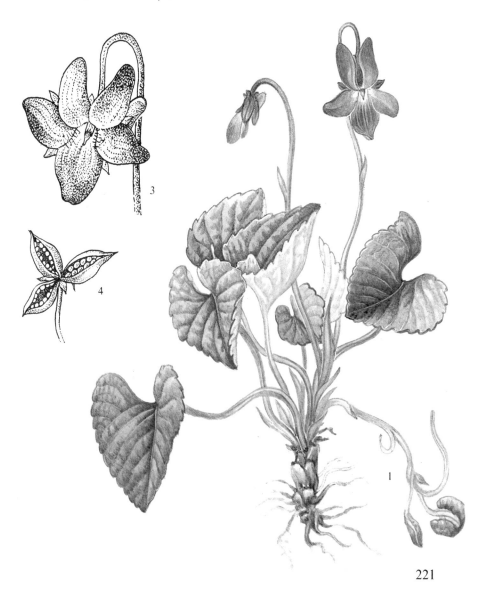

INDEX OF COMMON NAMES

INDEX OF LATIN NAMES

223